THE BEST OF BRIT
HOUSE H(

Katie Wood was born and educated in ~~~~~~~
read Communications and then English at university, and
worked as a freelance journalist before specializing in travel
in 1981. Author of many guidebooks, she has made a name
for herself both in Britain and internationally for her
practical, down-to-earth approach, and the quality of her
research.

Katie Wood continues to write freelance for the *Scotsman* and
several national magazines. She also contributes regularly to
television and radio travel programmes and is a fellow of the
Royal Geographical Society, undertaking specialist travel
consultancy work for airlines and tourist boards.

Married, with two children, Katie Wood lives in Perth,
Scotland.

KATIE WOOD

The Best of British Country House Hotels

Editorial Assistant: James Ogilvie

Fontana
An Imprint of HarperCollinsPublishers

In memory of Leslie Wood

Fontana
An Imprint of HarperCollins*Publishers*,
77–85 Fulham Palace Road,
Hammersmith, London W6 8JB

First published by Fontana 1989
This second edition first published 1991
9 8 7 6 5 4 3 2 1

ISBN 0 00 637734 3

Set in Linotron Palatino

Printed in Great Britain by
HarperCollinsManufacturing Glasgow

CONTENTS

Northern England

Wales

Central England

East Anglia

The Midlands

London

South-east England

South-west England

The Channel Islands

INTRODUCTION

A weekend stay in a Country House Hotel is for many the most pleasant and civilized way of getting away for a short break. It is wonderful to see so many of this type of British hotel enjoying their renaissance in recent years, having adapted to the times and opened their doors to the public, either as 'Open Houses' or, better still, as de luxe Country House Hotels where almost anybody can spend a few days amid the sort of surroundings normally only enjoyed by the super-rich or aristocracy.

The sheer indulgence in store for you in a Country House Hotel weekend is wonderful. It is a chance to step back in time and spoil yourself with a 'Brideshead-style' existence you didn't think was possible in the 1990s and, for a few days at least, to see how the other half lives. Surprisingly this treat (worth far more in terms of enjoyment and relaxation than numerous weeks in the sun-drenched Costas) need not cost such a prohibitive sum that it must be the preserve only of the very rich. Young professionals account for a substantial share of the Country House weekend-break market, and the recently retired are another significant group treating themselves to breaks in these houses. And quite right too. For the same price as a room and dinner in one of the large, business-orientated hotel chains, where the furnishings, food, atmosphere and staff's smiles are all decidedly on the plastic side, you can drive an hour or so into the country and spend your time in one of these beautiful old, historic houses and enjoy the luxuries and special touches of a bygone era – the fresh linen sheets, the quality toiletries in your bathroom, flowers in the bedroom, views of the countryside from the window, home-produced food and courteous service.

Everyone has at least three or four special occasions during the year – birthdays, anniversaries and family celebrations – and it's at these times that it really matters where you eat out, and what type of weekend you have. It is for this very reason that

I've put this book together. The hotels listed are not cheap, but for special occasions they *are* value for money.

We are very privileged in Britain to have such a fine collection of Country House Hotels. Our own particular history has left us this legacy, and I feel it is important that we patronize these houses so that they are not forced to close their doors and admit defeat to either the taxman, or escalating renovation costs. Few of these houses make large profits as hotels: their overheads are far greater than the bed-factories in towns and cities which pick up passing trade and have lucrative deals with travelling executives from large companies. Country House Hotels often depend on word of mouth bringing people to their doors, and then they rely on people coming back again. The fact that so many guests do, and then become hooked on Country House breaks, says a lot to recommend them.

Keeping a historic house watertight, heated and appropriately furnished, and maintaining staff who care about the house and the guests, is a costly affair, and while I'm not suggesting we should patronize these hotels out of a sense of duty or charity, I do think they deserve our special attention, and that, ideally, everyone should experience a Country House weekend at least once or twice a year.

Before I'm accused of an overdose of patriotism it must be said that our European neighbours, notably the French, Italians and Germans, do have their share of châteaux, villas and fine old schlöss operating as de luxe hotels. However, by comparison with British Country Houses they are few, and they can be exorbitantly expensive. They really *are* the preserve of the wealthy. Only the rich German industrialist could afford to treat his wife to a weekend in Schloss Buehlerhoehe, or the baron afford to take his favoured one to Villa San Michele, outside Florence, because their respective bed and breakfast prices are around £250–300 and that's before dinner! Conversely, our hotels are within financial reach of most people, even if it's just for the usually very reasonable set-dinners on offer, or the special winter-break weekends which many houses run out of season.

It is in the kitchens of the old English manor houses and Scottish castles that our country's finest young chefs are working and training, and the *nouvelle cuisine* which has transformed Britain's culinary reputation owes more to the likes of Kinnaird, Cliveden and Gidleigh Park than Langan's and the Savoy.

With the dramatic rise in popularity of Country House Hotel weekends (they now account for well over a thousand million pounds' worth of the British tourist trade), many hotels make claims to be 'Country Houses', but I have employed quite exacting standards as to what qualifies and what doesn't. Inglenook-fireplaces, converted in the 1970s, obviously reproduction 'antique' furnishings, gas-fuelled coal fires and fake brass, pleasant as they may be, are *not* the stuff of real Country House Hotels. To qualify for inclusion in this guide a house has to be the genuine article – a real country estate or house converted tastefully into a Country House Hotel. It must have high standards of accommodation, an outstanding restaurant, and be the sort of place where wedding nights might be spent.

Every hotel has been vetted by a team of professional travel journalists, with hundreds of hotel visits under their belts. All the tricks of the trade have been looked for and we think this guide is completely objective. No hotelier can buy his way in, and no advertising is taken.

This book contains, in my opinion, the best Country House Hotels in the UK at the time of publication. They are all places where I feel a memorable dinner or special weekend can be spent. Every establishment is vetted carefully, and everything from the cleanliness of the kitchens to the quality of the face cloths is taken into consideration. My research team and I are always open to new ideas, and any book like this lays itself wide open to criticism. It is almost inevitable some of you will disagree with my choices, or will hit a bad day in one of the hotels listed, but overall I hope this guide will be a useful addition to your bookshelf and will offer suggestions which lead to some marvellous meals and memorable weekends.

Colour photographs have been included in this edition to show off a selection of houses at their best, and there is a black and white line drawing of each house to give you an idea of what to expect, pointing out the architectural features of the buildings, without taking away too much from the moment you first see the house yourself, which is usually a very pleasant treat. The written description will tell you all you need to know about the house and should whet your appetite for it, while again still leaving some of the tiny minor details as surprises for when you arrive.

The country has been divided into seven regions: Scotland; Northern England; Central England; Wales; London Area; Southern England and the Channel Islands. Each hotel has been categorized into its price bracket. These are: up to £100; £100–£150; over £150. This is the price for two for dinner, bed and breakfast. Unless otherwise stated all the hotels have stressed to me the need to book ahead in high season (June to September), and unless we state to the contrary children and pets should be allowed, but it is always advisable to check with the hotel before departing.

Overall marks out of ten are awarded and displayed at the top of each entry. The final mark comes from the percentages awarded for the five categories by which the hotels were graded. These were Food, Service, Decor, Atmosphere and Facilities.

Each category is divided into sub-headings. Food is marked for taste, presentation, value for money and originality. Decor for the overall effect, authenticity to the style of the house and state of repair. Service is marked for efficiency and friendliness, and any special little touches added for the guest's convenience. Atmosphere was considered as an overall feeling, taking into account all of the other criteria. Do the guests feel at home, or is there an uncomfortable, stiff formality to the hotel? Have they a maître d' quietly orchestrating things or is the service erratic? Do you feel like a guest at a Country House weekend, or is it very obviously a paying hotel? Any jarring points? Overall, is it a happy place, offering value for money on all counts?

Facilities are marked more on presentation than on a strict count of what is or is not on offer. Hence a ten-bedroomed house with no more than a pool room and extensive grounds loses no marks to its neighbour boasting thirty bedrooms with jacuzzis and a whole leisure complex at its disposal. Assuming the basics for comfort and enjoyment are all there (as they are in all hotels listed in this guide), it is more a case of the use to which the facilities are put. It is points off for having beautiful grounds which have been allowed to fall into disrepair, or for sacrificing a library to make a sauna and swimming pool. At all times the Country House tradition has been considered. You can find hotels with every available facility you can think of up and down the country, but that's not what this book is about.

Any outstanding extras are mentioned in the text, but overall when you're looking at the hotel's mark, bear in mind the points outlined here.

A number of new entries appear in this extensively revised and updated version of *The Best of British Country House Hotels*. In addition, the list of contents at the front of the book now includes references to each hotel's nearest main town. The last edition included a number of criticisms of certain hotels, and it is gratifying to record that in many cases these drawbacks have been attended to. If there is one criticism that we feel deserves attention from the Country House Hotel industry today it is the provision of more comprehensive menus for the increasing number of vegetarians.

I sincerely hope you enjoy these special places. Please feel free to write to me with your comments on the hotels mentioned, and with any suggestions of your own. Address your correspondence to:

Katie Wood
Best of British Country House Hotels
Fontana Paperbacks
HarperCollins Publishers
77–85 Fulham Palace Road
London W6 8JB

Dress

As a rule, formal or smart evening dress is required for the dining rooms of all the hotels listed in this guide. Dinner jackets and long dresses are not compulsory in any, though guests at Cliveden (see p. 256) are encouraged to dress in this manner, as it is in keeping with the formal style of the house. The minimum accepted dress is jacket, collar and tie for a gent, and a dress for a lady; and this is required in all hotels listed.

Much of the pleasure in visiting a Country House comes from the after-breakfast stroll through the grounds, and for this a pair of wellington boots or stout walking shoes are invariably necessary. Irrespective of the season, you will come across muddy corners in the estate grounds, and when visiting between October and April waterproof clothing and footwear really is an essential if you are to have pleasure in exploring the grounds at all. Some hotels thoughtfully provide umbrellas, raincoats and even the odd pair of boots, but it's best to pack your own in the boot of the car, just in case. Many of the old estates date back to the period when specimen decorative trees were being introduced from abroad and consequently there are many fine examples of exotic and rare species in the grounds. If you are particularly interested in gardening, try to visit the house through the week and seek out the gardener for a chat. (If you're very lucky and are returning home that day or very soon after, you may be allowed to take cuttings from some of the more unusual plants for your own garden!)

Children

Many Country House Hotels take the unfortunate view that children are not welcome. The reasons they quote are invariably those of safety for their antique furnishings and disturbance to the other guests, many of whom, they say, go there to escape the noise and problems of family life. There is some justice in all this, but personally, as a mother of two young children myself, I do baulk at this Victorian 'seen and not heard' attitude. If the ground rules are laid out from the start – no under 12s in the dining room, any damages to be paid for, and so on – I do not see why children should be treated as outcasts. They are, after all, our next generation, and if they are not taught how to behave in civilized surroundings from an early age, how can we expect them to grow into balanced adults? This custom is rarely practised in the de luxe hotels of continental Europe, I'm happy to say. Particularly infuriating is the habit that some hotels have of allowing dogs, but not children. The little pooches can even be seen in the dining rooms! Personally I find few things more off-putting than to watch an overfed lap-dog being passed scraps from the plate by a doting owner, and I think priorities have become decidedly confused when one can't bring a baby into the breakfast room, but the dog can come to dinner.

All the hotels I list as accepting children will do so. Those which specify that they will not are very unlikely to change their policy.

Hotel reports

In many reports I have listed the house specialities or sample dishes to give an indication of the style and quality of the cuisine to be expected in the house. I cannot absolutely guarantee, however, that these particular dishes will be on the menu when you visit. If there is a dish you particularly want, phone or write ahead and request that it be made available for you. Vegetarian dishes can be prepared at all the houses, though if it is one with a smaller kitchen, or one which normally operates a table d'hôte menu only, please phone or write ahead.

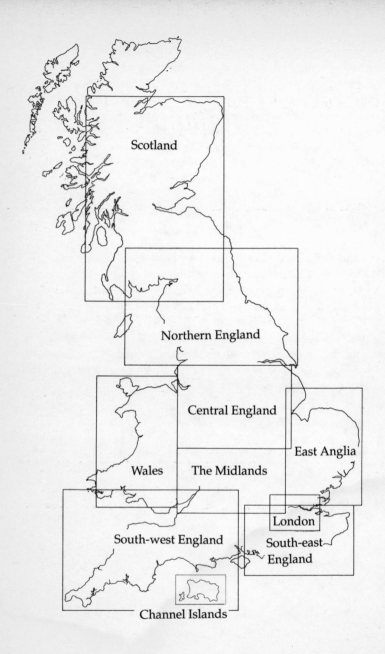

Scotland

Northern England

Central England

Wales

The Midlands

East Anglia

South-west England

London

South-east
England

Channel Islands

Scotland

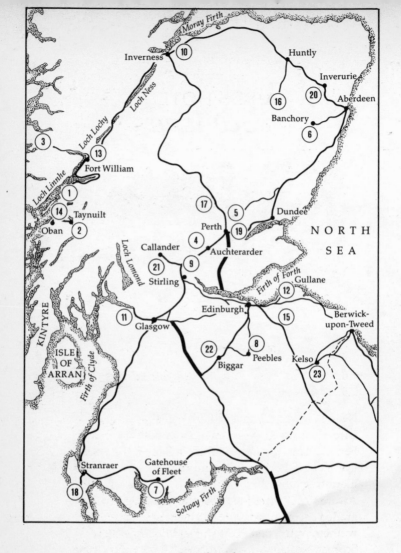

Scotland

1 Airds Hotel
2 Ardanaiseig
3 Arisaig House
4 Auchterarder House
5 Ballathie House
6 Banchory Lodge Hotel
7 Cally Palace
8 Cringletie House

9 Cromlix House
10 Culloden House
11 Gleddoch House
12 Greywalls
13 Inverlochy Castle
14 Isle of Eriska
15 Johnstounburn House
16 Kildrummy Castle

17 Kinnaird
18 Knockinaam Lodge
19 Murrayshall
20 Pittodrie House
21 Roman Camp
22 Shieldhill
23 Sunlaws House

AIRDS HOTEL

Address Port Appin, Appin, Argyll PA38 4DF
Tel: 063173 236 Fax: 063173 535

Nearest towns Oban and Fort William.
Directions Twenty-five miles from both Oban and
Fort William; the hotel is three miles off the A828
overlooking Lock Linnhe and the Morvern
mountain range.
Awards AA ** (red) plus rosette; Egon Ronay Star
graded recommendation; Michelin starred;
winners of the first Scottish Field/Bollinger Best
Scottish Restaurant Award; 1986 Good Food Guide
Scottish Hotel of the Year; member of Relais et
Châteaux 1988; chef Betty Allen was Scotland's
first, and so far only, female Chef Laureate of the
British Academy of Gastronomes.
Open from mid-March until mid-November.

Price for dinner, with wine, bed and breakfast for two – over £150.
Credit cards None accepted.
Children over 5 are welcomed, but dogs are not allowed. The hotel is unsuitable for disabled persons.
Overall mark out of ten 8½

For nearly three centuries the Airds Hotel has stood as a welcoming Ferry Inn by the village of Port Appin, overlooking the majestic Loch Linnhe. Current owners Eric and Betty Allen left Edinburgh some years ago and managed to transform the dull old inn into one of Argyll's most private Country Houses without destroying the wonderful eighteenth-century atmosphere. Although a number of standard concessions to modern-day luxury have deliberately been passed over in order to keep that atmosphere intact, you will receive a warm personal welcome and have an enviable opportunity to genuinely switch off and relax without worrying too much about the rest of the world.

There are fifteen bedrooms in all, each with private facilities, and comfortably, if not ostentatiously, furnished. Rather honestly, the owners say, 'We have no special facilities other than peace and quiet and good food.' The Airds' three large public rooms are spacious and comfortable; one is a particularly attractive sun-lounge during the summer months – and a perfect retreat from the chilly Argyll autumn evenings if you choose to visit towards the end of the hotel's annual season.

Eating in the Airds' intimate dining room, with its glorious views far across the loch, will undoubtedly be one of the highlights of your visit to this hotel. Indeed, such is the reputation of the hotel's fine cooking that it is the principal reason, even before the prospect of enjoying the uninterrupted solitude of the surrounding countryside is taken into consideration, for many visitors returning year after year.

Smoking is not permitted in the dining room and there is approximately a four-to-one ratio between residents and non-residents in the dining room at any one time. The restaurant has one of the best reputations of any Country House in Scotland and advance booking is strongly urged.

Presentation and service are immaculate, and dinner is served at a single sitting around 8 p.m. to ensure everything can be cooked and served as freshly as possible. The style of food is distinctly Scottish, although subtle continental influences are obvious on the fine-grey card menus which are changed daily. All the food is locally produced and rigorously selected to ensure only the finest cuts of meat and fish are prepared. Most of the vegetables are grown in the large kitchen garden which the hotel owners look after themselves.

Locally caught seafood features mainly on the list of starters, although Betty's magnificent Poached Fillets of Sole with Prawns and Vermouth Cream Sauce is a mouthwatering exception on the main course options. Other recommended specialities are Breast of Pigeon with Thyme and Juniper Sauce and Ravioli of Lobster and Prawns served with a Caviar Sauce. All meals can be complemented with a wine selected from over 350 on the shrewdly prepared list. Although house wines start from under £10 a bottle, the list includes most European favourites and some of the rarest modern wines available anywhere in Scotland – at a price, of course, but well worth the once-off extravagance to go with that special meal.

The hotel is well located for touring historic Argyllshire, and nearby attractions include the spectacular Glen Coe, the famous pass from the Moor of Rannoch to Loch Leven and site of the Glen Coe massacre in 1692. A poignant memorial stands in memory of the murdered Macdonalds and the area now acts as the beautiful setting for more peaceful activities including rock climbing and skiing. You can also visit Castle Stalker, a Stewart hunting lodge used by King James IV before the Battle of Flodden Field in 1513. Other attractions include day trips to Fort William, or Oban, a busy little seaside resort from where you can sail to Mull for the day.

ARDANAISEIG

Address Kilchrenan, by Taynuilt, Argyll PA35 1HE
Tel: 08663 333 Fax: 08663 222

Nearest town Village of Kilchrenan, or the larger
Taynuilt a few miles further away.

Directions Turn south off the A85 at Taynuilt on to
the B845 to Kilchrenan. Head left at the Ardanaiseig
signpost when you reach Kilchrenan and the hotel
is four miles further on.

A member of the **Pride of Britain** consortium.

Awards AA *** (red) and rosette for food; Michelin
three (red) turrets; Egon Ronay 76% and star for
food; American Hideaway report: Scottish Hotel of
the Year 1986.

Open from Easter until mid-October.

No special breaks, but the hotel offers a reduced
two or more nights rate throughout the season.

Price for dinner, with wine, bed and breakfast for
two – over £150.

Credit cards Access, Visa, Diners and Amex.

Ardanaiseig is not suitable for the disabled and does not allow children under the age of eight.
Overall mark out of ten 7½

Nestling in the heart of mountainous Argyllshire, Ardanaiseig is steeped in history and surrounded by acres of woodland and scrub. For centuries the Clan Campbell owned and controlled most of the region and it was a member of that clan, Colonel James Archibald Campbell, who built the present house in 1834. He spent over two years just laying out the grounds and planting the trees, many of which are fine examples today, before the house itself was started. The house was built by William Burn, who was one of the leading architects of his time, and one of just four appointed to carry out Robert Adam's unfinished plans for Edinburgh's New Town in the decades after his death in 1793.

Sunday mornings at Ardanaiseig always witnessed an intriguing family ritual during the years when Colonel Campbell was in residence. He would sternly line up his ample collection of daughters and then choose one or two to row him across Loch Awe to church at Cladich. The rest of the sizeable family would follow in a flotilla of smaller boats at a discreet distance behind the head of the household!

Colonel Campbell died in 1879, by which time he had helped form the then 100,000 strong National Union of Agricultural Workers which later became the powerful National Union of Farmers. A hundred years later, the modern NUF still has a very considerable membership in Scotland alone. Ardanaiseig was sold in 1880 after the old man's death and, curiously, occupied in turn by two successive Members of Parliament for Argyll before being bought by the present owners in 1963 and transformed into a Country House Hotel.

Very little of the original interior has been altered structurally, apart from the addition of a few extra bathrooms and fire safety requirements, and as a result the owners' attempt to retain the atmosphere of a private house has largely succeeded. All three public rooms, including the airy dining room, have fine views across the loch. The hotel has a particularly attractive drawing

7

room, with a huge bay window looking out across the grounds and allowing you to savour every moment spent enjoying the views. Tastefully decorated, the drawing room has a number of comfortable armchairs, a good grand piano and a constant supply of fresh flowers; almost too inviting to ignore.

Ardanaiseig has a total of fourteen bedrooms; twelve doubles and two singles. All are well furnished, centrally heated and with their own private facilities including colour television and direct-dial telephone. Rooms to the back of the house have the best views across the loch and up towards Ben Lui. The magnificent surrounding thirty-two-acre grounds are one of Ardanaiseig's most attractive features, famous for their rhodo-dendrons and azaleas.

The hotel's dining room has traditional decor, candle-lit in the evenings, and pink table linen accompanies the silverware at each meal. The style of cooking is best described as modern British with a strong emphasis on traditional Scottish specialities like Fillet of Beef Argyll and Fillet of Wild Salmon. A speciality of chef Martin Vincent is his 'Symphony of Seafoods', a delicious array of locally caught seafood gently poached then blended with a creamy Noilly Prat sauce flavoured with saffron and chervil. A number of speciality dishes have an additional charge of a few pounds, but the chef makes the bold pledge on the menu that, subject to a few days' notice, he will be pleased to produce any dish of your choice.

The hotel offers a wide range of outdoor sporting facilities for residents; tennis, croquet, fishing, boating and clay pigeon shooting are all available throughout the season. Nearby attractions include Oban; Glen Coe, one of Scotland's most dramatic glens; and the Mull of Kintyre, made famous by Paul McCartney's worldwide 1978 hit record of the same name. Loch Awe and Loch Etive are also within easy reach and both are beautiful whatever the season.

ARISAIG HOUSE

Address Beasdale, Arisaig, Invernesshire PH39 4NR
Tel: 06875 622 Fax: 06875 626

Nearest town Fort William.
Directions Drive west from Fort William on the
A830, then clearly signposted after thirty miles.
Awards AA *** (red); Michelin three red turrets plus
red M; BTA commended Country House Hotel;
Scottish Tourist Board Highly Commended four
Crowns; Egon Ronay 75% highly commended.
Open from mid-March until November, excluding
August and September.
Special terms for stays of five days or over provided
booking is made direct to the hotel.
Price for dinner, with wine, bed and breakfast for
two – over £150.
Credit cards Access, Visa.
*The hotel is not suited for disabled persons; children over
ten are welcome. Dogs are not permitted.*
Overall mark out of ten 7½

Built in 1864 to the design of the great Victorian architect Philip Webb, Arisaig House is a splendid old mansion, ideally situated for touring the Western Highlands or nearby islands. Offering perfect peace and tranquillity combined with luxury service, Arisaig was completely rebuilt in 1937 by Ian Hamilton after being gutted by fire. One of the most appealing features of the hotel today is the 1930s 'time-warp' atmosphere which you can sense throughout the hotel and, above all, in the airy dining room.

Bonnie Prince Charlie is reputed to have hidden after the Battle of Culloden in a dank cave, still known as Charlie's Cave, located quite near the hotel. From there he met a small French frigate on a dark night in 1746 and escaped back to France with the help of some of his remaining countrymen. Few could have guessed at the time of this sad departure that he was destined to live there in exile from his native Scotland for the rest of his life.

As you approach Arisaig along the gravel driveway, you will be able to appreciate, for the first time during your stay here, the real beauty of the hotel's surrounding twenty acres of grounds. Arisaig is sheltered from the north and has sweeping views to the south and east of a great sea loch and mountains. At the height of summer the immediate garden area around the hotel is a delight, with broad terraces overlooking the gardens. Well-tended displays of azaleas, rhododendrons and countless varieties of wild shrubs stretch from the hotel's outer walls up to the fringes of natural woodland which quite completes this charming scene.

Three additional walled gardens can be explored by residents, and it is here that all the fresh flowers which decorate the hotel's public rooms are grown. The house as a whole is distinctly stylish and the two main public rooms, the Morning Room and the Drawing Room, have great windows to take advantage of the amazing views. Roaring log fires on those chilly autumn evenings are ideal to help you relax and enjoy your after-dinner coffee.

Arisaig has a total of fifteen bedrooms, including five master bedrooms. All have been individually designed to the specifications of current proprietors Ruth and John Smither, and offer private bathroom facilities, together with colour television and direct-dial telephone. Rooms have their own Scottish names – Nevis, Morar and so on – giving that little bit of extra individuality which is so sadly missed from more modern hotels in the same price bracket. All rooms offer particularly fine views of the surrounding woodland, sea loch or mountain, depending on which side of the house you find yourself.

One of Arisaig's most attractive features is its 1930s-style wood-panelled dining room. The food is based on first-class local produce with a touch of *nouvelle cuisine*; indeed, most of the vegetables on your evening dinner plate come from no further away than the hotel's own walled gardens, which are lovingly looked after by the proprietors.

Dinner is served from a recommended menu of five courses. Residents may select alternatives from within any given evening's prepared fare. Under Head Chef Matthew Burns the standard of food is quite superb and there is a particularly fine range of hors d'oeuvres. For a typical main course of Duck Breast with Green Peppercorn sauce or Fillet of Sole Vincent Bourrel you may care to whet your appetite beforehand with Smoked Venison with Asparagus and Fromage Blanc, Salad of Smoked Mussels, Oysters and Avocado, or even Bavarois of Smoked Salmon, Cheese and Cucumber. Dinner includes a fish course: perhaps locally caught pan-fried Scallops set on a dill and Vermouth sauce or a Roulade of Turbot, Salmon and garden herbs on a butter sauce. There is a comprehensive wine list with 100 or so bottles from which to select.

Attractions include day trips to nearby Mallaig, the northern end of the famous West Highland railway line; a visit to the Isle of Skye – regular car ferries make the short crossing from Mallaig to Armadale; and boat trips across to the smaller islands of Canna, Rhum, Eigg or Muck from the village of Arisaig.

4

AUCHTERARDER HOUSE

Address Auchterarder, near Gleneagles, Perthshire
PH3 1DZ
Tel: 0764 63636 Fax: 0764 62939

Nearest town Auchterarder
Directions Auchterarder House is fifty miles from
Edinburgh and sixty from Glasgow. Head for
either Perth or Stirling, whichever is nearer to your
departure point, and then follow signs for
Auchterarder. Following the B8062 from the main
street in Auchterarder, the hotel is about 1½ miles
along the road. The entrance is through gates by
the lodge house.
A member of the **Prestige Hotel** consortium.
Awards 1989 Winner of the Caithness Glass/Taste
of Scotland award for Best Overall Excellence; Egon
Ronay 74%; Scottish Tourist Board five Crowns –
highly commended.
Open throughout the year.
Special breaks Theme weekends, private house
parties, and longer stay discounts available.

Note No special rates apply over Christmas and New Year, or the Easter weekend.
Price for dinner, with wine, bed and breakfast for two – over £150
Credit cards Access, Visa, Amex, Diners, Mastercharge and Carte Bleu.
No children under the age of twelve are allowed.
Overall mark out of ten 9

Within a couple of miles of the world-famous five-star Gleneagles Hotel lies a much smaller and more intimate Country House Hotel offering similar standards of luxury at substantially lower rates. Auchterarder House is one of the best-value options in central Scotland especially if you can afford the time to travel outwith the main summer months.

Auchterarder itself is an ancient Royal Burgh which was ideally situated on the road which leads from Scone Palace, home for generations of Scottish monarchs in medieval times and before, to historic Stirling Castle. By the early nineteenth century half of the burgh was in the possession of Lieutenant-Colonel James Hunter who commissioned Scottish architect William Burn to design an impressive new mansion house for him.

Within a year, by 1832, the oldest part of the present hotel was completed and today visitors still marvel at their first sight of Burn's asymmetrical two-storey design, with its crow-stepped gables built in the old Jacobean style, as they draw up to the front of the building. The south wing and terraces were added towards the end of the last century, by which time the house was no longer owned by the Hunter family, and the interior modelled in a rich Renaissance style, with elegant Victorian overtones, which is how it basically remains today. James Reid, the new owner after the Hunter family sold the house, was the great railway magnate responsible for a huge railroad construction firm which supplied locomotives throughout the world. He gave much of his wealth to the City of Glasgow in the form of donations of art treasures, and a statue of James Reid can be seen in Glasgow's Springburn Park.

The sumptuous interior of Auchterarder House is emphasized

by fine wood panelling and ornate ceilings in all the public rooms, and a number of the bedrooms. All the public rooms are furnished with reproduction Victorian furniture offering romantic, old-style comfort for even the most discerning. Entertainment for guests is unpretentious. Auchterarder's library provides a wide range of reading material, the grounds offer a beautiful setting for croquet, and golfers can practise their skills on the pitch and putt hole. In the evening Ian Brown, the resident owner, can often be found at the piano, giving an impromptu concert of favourite music.

The main dining room is arranged to seat twenty-five people and has a distinct Scottish atmosphere. The quality of food served is very high, with a strong Scottish emphasis. Pre-prandial canapés, and post-dinner coffee, served with a *petit four*, are complimentary and the impressive à la carte menu will cost you between £23 and £50, depending whether you have two or five courses.

The hotel has six main-wing bedrooms, six turret-wing bedrooms and two courtyard suites. All the bedrooms are individually named and furnished to the highest standards with colour television, telephone, trouser press and so forth. A few display some rather out-of-place ornaments here and there, but the overall impression is good. All have their own private bathroom facilities which include a number of interesting 'extras', including a good range of soaps and complimentary toiletries. Nearby attractions include Scone Palace, where kings of Scotland were crowned for eight centuries; Glamis Castle, childhood home of Queen Elizabeth, the Queen Mother; Blair Castle; Strathallan Aircraft Museum; Crieff glassworks; the natural splendour of the Trossachs; and a number of major whisky distilleries.

5

BALLATHIE HOUSE

Address Kinclaven by Stanley, Perthshire PH1 4QN
Tel: 025083 268 Fax: 025083 396

Nearest town Perth.
Directions From Perth, take the A9 northwards.
After two miles take the B9000 through Stanley,
turning right at the sign for Kinclaven. Ballathie is
on the right-hand side after a short distance.
A member of **Best Western and Scotland's Heritage**
hotels.
Awards Scottish Tourist Board four Crowns –
recommended.
Open throughout the year.
Special breaks Spring and autumn special terms
available for a minimum of two days.
Activity/interest packages also available.
Price for dinner, with wine, bed and breakfast for
two – £100–£150.
Credit cards Amex, Visa, Diners and Access.
Children are welcome. Dogs are admitted to some
bedrooms only, at a cost of £1 and by prior arrangement.
The hotel has accommodation suitable for the less able and
disabled.
Overall mark out of ten 8

The first thing that strikes you about Ballathie is its superb setting. The approach to this baronial house is a delight, particularly in early summer when the rhododendrons are a riot of pink and purple hues. One's first glimpse of the hotel from the tree-lined drive reveals a solid and imposing mansion, its grey-slated pinnacles softened by a covering of spreading creepers reaching up from below. Originally built in 1850, Ballathie remained in private hands until as recently as 1971. Happily, its subsequent conversion to a hotel and later refurbishment was sympathetic both to the architecture and internal style, compromising nothing in achieving the quintessence of a Scottish baronial hall. Today, Ballathie enjoys a deserved reputation as one of Scotland's most distinctive and outstanding Country House Hotels.

Within the hotel itself, its oak stairways, panelling and floors create an air of solid grandeur, softened somewhat by the informality of its relaxed decor and the presence of log fires in its public rooms. With its ornate ceilings and muted walls Ballathie's elegant drawing room gives fine views out over the riverside lawns. After breakfast it draws guests to observe the activity on the River Tay as they sip their morning coffee; during the evening it becomes a retreat to relive the day's memories over a malt whisky or a liqueur.

Ballathie's twenty-seven bedrooms are finished to the highest standard. Many display antique furniture – including four-poster beds – within their pastel-shaded walls, while all possess superb views over the surrounding Perthshire countryside. Its 'Premier' rooms are large and stylish, while its 'Standard' rooms display a more intimate, cottage-style appearance. Every room has its own private bath and/or shower, while great care is taken in providing details, like hairdryers, trouser presses, drinks and fresh fruit, which give that all-important personal touch so welcoming to arriving visitors. The 'River Suite' and two further bedrooms on the ground floor are designed with disabled guests in mind, having direct access both to the driveway and to the hotel grounds. Next to the main house, the 'Sporting Lodge' – originally designed for hunting, shooting and fishing parties –

has rooms finished to a simpler style, but with facilities similar to those of the main house.

With its ornate ceiling and walls, the dining room provides a fitting setting in which to enjoy Ballathie's delightful cuisine. The hotel uses only the freshest produce for its menus, and meals are prepared with care and imagination. As one might expect, Tay salmon features prominently, while local game, Scottish beef, lamb and seafoods are all represented in the fare, which changes daily. Timbale of Smoked Salmon centred with Hot Scallops on a light herb dressing makes a mouthwatering starter, while Escalopes of Veal and Venison Sauté with freshly ground Juniper berries and flamed in gin provides a memorable main dish (unless of course you're a total salmon fanatic, in which case the opportunity to sample Darne of River Tay Salmon lightly poached in Court Bouillon and glazed under a hollandaise sauce should not be forgone). While the menu is essentially traditional in format, special diets can be catered for by arrangement. Ballathie's creditable wine list, of international choice, ranges in price from only £7 to over £35 for a bottle of claret, for example.

The hotel has a reputation for being something of a mecca for fishermen and women when the salmon are running. It does, however, offer much more on the leisure side than simply being a base for fishing alone. Croquet, putting, tennis and clay pigeon shooting are all offered, while for those who prefer quieter pursuits, riverside walks can be enjoyed without the need to leave the hotel's extensive grounds. It is best to book field sports well in advance with the Ballathie Estate Office, as demand in season is high.

As a touring centre Ballathie is well placed for visiting the mid-Scotland towns of Perth, Dunkeld and Blairgowrie. Further afield, Royal Deeside, Speyside, Aviemore, Inverness, Fort William and the west coast are typical and rewarding day excursions.

6

BANCHORY LODGE HOTEL

Address Banchory, Kincardineshire AB3 3HS
Tel: 03302 2625

Nearest town Banchory.
Directions Travel eighteen miles west of Aberdeen
on the A93. The hotel is situated on Royal Deeside,
beside the River Dee, at the confluence of the River
Feugh.
Awards AA *** (red) graded since 1977; RAC Blue
Ribbon award ***; British Tourist Authority
commended; Scottish Tourist Board four Crowns –
highly commended.
Open from the beginning of February until mid-
December.
Price for dinner, with wine, bed and breakfast for
two – up to £100.
Credit cards Access, Visa, Diners, Amex, Carte
Blanche.
*The hotel welcomes children and dogs, but is unsuitable
for disabled guests.*
Overall mark out of ten 7

A building of some description is reputed to have stood on

the site of the Banchory Lodge Hotel for over one-and-a-half
thousand years. Saint Ternan brought Christianity to the area
of Banchory in the fifth century AD, teaching the local Picts the
ways of European agriculture, arts and crafts, and building a
monastery at the point where the rivers Feugh and Dee met.
Ternan's white-coloured circular palace, or 'Ban Choire', stood
as the beginning of modern Banchory.

Over the centuries the old monastery decayed and crumbled
away and a modest lodge first appeared in its place. It was here
that mail coaches used to halt while the horses were rested and
watered before the last stretch up Deeside proper. A ferryman's
house stood on or near the site of the present hotel long before
the bridge over the Dee was built at Banchory.

Banchory Lodge as you will find it today, was restored and
greatly enlarged in the eighteenth century by General William
Burnett. He eventually retired here after a lifetime of faithful
service as equerry to both King George III, who died in 1820,
and his son George IV, who reigned over Great Britain a further
ten years before his own death in 1830. The Lodge used to
include the lands of Arbeadie on which most of the present
town of Banchory, and the immediate surrounding area, is built.

Present owners, Dugald and Margaret Jaffray, have made a
number of substantial improvements to the property since they
bought it in 1966. Even so, a modest Georgian atmosphere still
prevails and much of the authentic period charm can still be
appreciated. Open log fires and magnificent flower arrangements enhance the two spacious public lounges which offer
grand views out across the River Dee which runs through the
grounds of the hotel. Indeed, the Dee is one of the finest salmon
rivers in the world and fishing is one of the central attractions
of the Banchory Lodge. Bear in mind that the salmon fishing
season only runs from 1 February to 30 September in this part
of Scotland.

The main dining room has a traditional design and is furnished with authentic Victorian tables and chairs. Lunch and
dinner are served in this room and up to eighty can be seated
at any one time. Breakfast is served in a smaller oak-panelled
dining room, which is also available for private functions.

Banchory Lodge has a brigade of chefs and cooks and preparation, planning and cooking are supervised by the owners. The table d'hôte menu offers a good range and is prepared almost exclusively from local produce. The range of starters is imaginative and the main courses, including, of course, Dee salmon, and roast beef are good. When you reach the dessert course you are really spoiled for choice with almost a dozen options ranging from Water Melon in Ginger Beer to Irish Coffee Gateau. Whatever the course, the size of the portions is always more than generous.

Banchory Lodge has a total of twenty-four bedrooms, all with colour television and private facilities. Three offer the added luxury of four-poster beds for that touch of romance. Eight bedrooms have been built in the south-facing wing, the most recent structural addition to the hotel. Two of the three four-poster rooms are in this wing, and the remaining six rooms have both a single and a double bed, making them ideal for families.

Nearby attractions are plentiful. Within an easy drive you can reach Crathes Castle, Craigievar Castle, Kildrummy Castle, Dunottar Castle, Drum Castle, Braemar Castle, Pitmedden Gardens, Leith Hall, Haddo House and, of course, the Royal Family's Scottish residence at Balmoral, the grounds of which are open throughout the summer when the family are not in residence.

CALLY PALACE

Address Gatehouse of Fleet, Dumfries and
Galloway DG7 2DL
Tel: 0557 814341 Fax: 0557 814522

Nearest town Gatehouse of Fleet.
Directions From Dumfries, take the A75 west
towards Stranraer. Turning off the bypass towards
Gatehouse you will see the driveway to the Cally
Palace clearly signposted on your left.
Awards AA and RAC **** graded; Scottish Tourist
Board four Crowns – highly commended.
Open from March until late December.
Special breaks Weekend breaks from 1 October
until the end of May (excluding Christmas and
New Year period).
Price for dinner, with wine, bed and breakfast for
two – £100–£150.
Credit cards Only Visa.
*Facilities are available to accommodate disabled guests;
children of any age and dogs are welcome.*
Overall mark out of ten 8

Hidden away in the heart of southern Scotland, Cally Palace
really is the 'complete resort' it claims to be in its impressive

glossy brochures. An unhurried atmosphere and elegant private grounds are assured, and if you have never before explored this part of Scotland then a stay at this particular Country House Hotel would be a good starting point.

The hotel has a long and interesting history, with its origins dating back to the mid-seventeenth century when the village of Gatehouse itself first began to grow up. The Murray family who first built the present hotel owned it right up until the start of the Second World War. The current family representative, Mrs Murray Usher, still owns an impressive town hotel in Gatehouse, once frequented by Robert Burns.

Cally Palace really took shape in 1835 when the existing modest country mansion underwent a great deal of alteration and improvement. A portico was added to the front of the house and four massive granite monoliths were erected, creating the impressive frontal exterior which can still be seen. The stone was quarried from Craigdeus near the town of Newton Stewart some fifteen miles away. It is hard to believe that the now quiet little village of Gatehouse contained, at that time, no less than four cotton factories, several tanneries, a brickworks, a soap factory, a brass foundry, a wine company, a busy brewery, and even a prosperous ship-building and repair yard.

Two huge oak front doors are one of the hotel's most striking features as you draw up to it. Behind these magnificent reminders of former glory, lies the great marble entrance hall which is almost certain to make the first-time visitor take a step back in admiration. No brochure illustration can do justice to this marvellous public reception area. Indeed, the splendour enjoyed by earlier generations has been maintained throughout Cally Palace and it would be hard to criticize any aspect of the hotel's largely authentic period decor. All the spacious public rooms have intricately ornate ceilings, outsize marble fireplaces and reproduction period furniture. The main dining room was refurbished in 1987 in elegant blue and pink. Well over a hundred can be seated at any one time, so most of the year it remains surprisingly uncrowded. Cally Palace is one of the most popular 'society' choices for smart local weddings and as a conference location for those from further afield.

The hotel reckons about 95 per cent of their dinner guests are residents, which is a pity for non-residents staying nearby, considering the outstanding value of their four-course table d'hôte menu. Beef, one of Scotland's finest specialities (and Cally Palace is no exception), is a main course alternative every evening. Other recommended main dishes include Julienne of Chicken cooked in Lemon and Cream Sauce, finished with strips of smoked salmon, and Poached Fillet of Plaice served with a White Wine and Prawn Sauce. An à la carte menu and extensive wine list are also available.

The hotel has a total of fifty-five bedrooms, including seven suites, one family suite, and a sumptuous honeymoon suite. As you might expect, all rooms have private bathroom facilities, colour television, telephone and so forth. Residents may find the hotel's size rather intimidating as it is rather larger than the average Scottish Country House establishment, but where Cally Palace really comes into its own is when taken as a self-contained resort rather than 'just' a smart Country Hotel.

Offering itself as the perfect all-round retreat, the hotel has just installed an indoor pool with sauna, jacuzzi and solarium, and there are also facilities available for tennis, golf (or more leisurely putting), a large outdoor heated swimming pool, forest walks and bird-watching in the surrounding private grounds – and there's even a nursery to let those with young children have a real break for an hour or two.

Nearby attractions include the picturesque Galloway coast, with the towns of Dumfries, Castle Douglas, Kirkcudbright and Newton Stewart. Also within a short drive are three golf courses or you can visit Cardoness Castle, Dundrennan Abbey, Drum-lanrig Castle, and a number of places associated with Robert Burns in and around Dumfries.

CRINGLETIE HOUSE

Address Peebles, Peeblesshire EH45 8PL
Tel: 07213 233

Nearest town Peebles.
Directions From Peebles, Cringletie House is just
two miles north on the main A703 Edinburgh road.
Awards AA **; British Tourist Authority
commended; recommended by Egon Ronay, Ashley
Courtenay and the Hotel Collection.
Open from early March until 2 January.
Special breaks for stays of five days or more are
available for dinner, bed and breakfast inclusive.
Price for dinner, with wine, bed and breakfast –
£100–£150.
Credit cards Access and Visa.
Overall mark out of ten 8

Just twenty miles from Edinburgh, in the Scottish Borders, Cringletie House is ideally situated for touring most of east-central
and southern Scotland. A distinguished old red-sandstone
mansion house, Cringletie sits in twenty-eight acres of private

grounds and was originally designed by Scottish architect David Bryce in the middle of the last century. The pink stone house was built in 1861 for the Wolfe Murray family and, indeed, it was Colonel Alexander Murray Cringletie who accepted the surrender of Quebec after General Wolfe was killed.

All the hotel's public rooms are tastefully decorated in Victorian style, and furnished to a very high standard of comfort. The main lounge area is decorated with magnificent dark panels, and the Victorian portrait framed above the marble fireplace quite completes the period image. The house's former library has been turned into a second lounge bar area, and log fires are the order of the day in both public lounges whenever the east coast weather turns chilly. Views from this room are particularly attractive, stretching out far across the surrounding grounds. The bar is particularly well stocked with Scottish malt whiskies so you will probably never find a more relaxing setting in which to experiment with the drink Gaelic speakers aptly term 'the water of life'.

The dining room is another Victorian-style panelled room and seats a total of fifty people, about half of whom are non-residents at any one time. The present proprietors, Stanley and Aileen Maguire, have owned the hotel since 1971, and in that time have established a strong reputation for good cuisine with the emphasis on imaginative home-produced food. The full Scottish breakfasts are guaranteed to ensure you will not leave the table feeling hungry.

Aileen Maguire takes charge of the cooking herself and her distinctive home style has won an impressive number of awards over the last seventeen years. Much of the produce comes from Cringletie's huge two-acre kitchen garden. The range of hors d'oeuvres has a strong local flavour, including fresh Smoked Salmon and an interesting Mushroom Mousse baked in Cream. Mrs Maguire's expertise in the kitchen really comes into its own, however, when you sample her range of main course options. Traditional dishes like Roast Loin of Pork and Casseroled Haunch of Venison vie for your palate with a wider selection of more unusual house specialities. Two particular favourites are Lemon Stuffed Chicken Supreme with Cream Sauce and Baked

Monkfish with Cider and Mustard Sauce and Mozzarella Cheese. Sauces with intriguing alcohol bases feature prominently; you can have your Venison bathed with Guinness and Prunes, or your Lamb Kidney cooked in Brandy and Cream. One above-average touch is the fried banana which is served as a garnish to the Grilled Fillet of Sole St Lucia – coated in buttery coconut. After your choice of sweets, coffee can be taken in the lounge and is served with home-made *petits fours*.

Cringletie has a total of thirteen bedrooms, including one single, all with en suite bathroom facilities and television. Bedrooms are all different and each has a distinctive identity. One right at the upper corner of the house has a peculiar turret window, a very rare sight even in Country House Hotels. Advance booking is essential if this particular room appeals to you.

Nearby attractions are almost too numerous to name. First and foremost, of course, is the city of Edinburgh, about half an hour's drive away, with all that it has to offer. Local castles and stately homes within easy reach include Traquair House, Bowhill, Abbotsford (once home of Sir Walter Scott), Floors Castle (still home to the Duke of Roxburghe) and Thirlestane Castle. The surrounding countryside is among Scotland's finest and a few suggested local highlights which you can see near here are St Mary's Loch, Grey Mare's Tail and the Moorfoot hills.

CROMLIX HOUSE

Address Kinbuck, Dunblane, Perthshire FK15 9JT
Tel: 0786 822125

Nearest town Stirling.
Directions From both Glasgow and Edinburgh
follow the M9 to Dunblane then follow the B8033
to the village of Kinbuck. Cromlix House is half a
mile north of here and signposted.
A member of the **Pride of Britain** consortium.
Awards AA *** graded and rosette for food; 1984
Egon Ronay Hotel of the Year; 1986 Restaurant of the
Year award from *Decanter* magazine; 1988 Egon
Ronay Outstanding Wine List; 1989 Taste of
Scotland Best Country House Hotel; British Tourist
Authority commended hotel; Scottish Tourist
Board's highest commendation – five Crowns.
Open all year round.
Special breaks Bargain winter breaks available from
1 October; also Fly-Drive weekends throughout the
year.

Price for dinner, with wine, bed and breakfast for two – over £150.
Credit cards Access, Visa, Amex, Diners.
Not suitable for visitors with severe physical disability; children and dogs welcome.
Overall mark out of ten 9½

Some of the highest standards of international luxury combine with an elegant Country House atmosphere to make Cromlix one of the most outstanding Scottish hotels included in this guide. Originally built as a family house in 1880, Cromlix was altered and extended around the turn of the century. Much of the south-west of the house can be seen as it was when first occupied, and the Cromlix House which King Edward VII came to visit in 1908 is basically the modern-day hotel which awaits you.

The hotel stands on land which has been in the continuous ownership of the same family for an impressive five centuries. Formerly owned by the Hays and the Drummonds, the house and 5000-acre surrounding estate now belong to the related Edens. As you might expect, an abundance of outdoor activities, including tennis, riding, hill-walking, bird-watching, croquet, shooting (both clay and live game by prior arrangements) and fishing (trout, salmon and sea), is available on the estate.

The hotel has a number of elegant public rooms including three separate dining rooms. One such room, the library, can accommodate up to twelve people for private dinners around a rather unusual round table. After-dinner liqueurs can be enjoyed in the same room around a log fire. The original family dining room can seat up to sixteen people separately or together as a party around one huge table.

The main dining room is the hotel's old drawing room, and offers superb views through the French windows across to the newly renovated conservatory, back lawns and wide gardens. Non-residents are welcome for dinner but advance booking is essential as Cromlix is generally full most of the year. The hotel's Victorian conservatory is a delight, and allows an extra twelve non-residents to be served for dinner.

Under chef Mark Salton the high standards of cooking at Cromlix embrace a mixture of many ideas and influences. It is not so much *nouvelle cuisine* as Country House or Modern Classic style, though the presentation is beautiful and the quality absolutely first class. The emphasis on freshness throughout the menu is very noticeable and much of the produce is grown or reared in the grounds around Cromlix.

A set menu is provided each night although alternatives are always available, and a strong point in the hotel's favour is the kitchen's ability to adapt to meet special dietary requirements. During the season, the hotel uses a wide variety of game from the surrounding estate, including hare, rabbit, pheasant, woodcock, venison and wild duck. Salmon and trout often come from estate lochs or nearby rivers. Two of the most popular main dishes at Cromlix are Breast of Duck in a Four Fruits Vinegar Sauce, Glazed Apples and Baby Vegetables, and Loin of Scottish Lamb, Charlotte of Aubergine, Gratin Dauphinoise and Rosemary Sauce. The hotel has a very comprehensive wine list, with over 400 vintages to suit all palates regardless of your choice of starter and main dish.

Cromlix House has a total of fourteen bedrooms, including eight suites which are all furnished to the highest standard with period-style pieces which enhance the atmosphere of Victorian luxury. A visiting correspondent wrote, in a profile of the hotel: 'I am still waiting to be persuaded that the Upper Turret at Cromlix is not the finest suite of rooms in Scotland.' As you might expect, bookings for the best suites are essential – at least nine months in advance.

Nearby attractions include the Stuart Strathearn glassworks; Doune Motor Museum; Loch Lomond (and loch cruises on the popular *Countess Fiona*); Blair Castle; Dunblane Cathedral; and of course, the cities of Edinburgh and Glasgow, and the town of Stirling, which can all be reached within an hour's drive.

10

CULLODEN HOUSE

Address Inverness, Invernesshire IY1 2NZ
Tel: 0463 790461

Nearest town Inverness.
Directions From Inverness or Nairn, take signs to
Culloden off the A96 Inverness/Nairn, adjacent to
Culloden village. Do *not* follow the Culloden signs
on the A9.
A member of the **Prestige Hotels** consortium.
Awards AA **** graded; Egon Ronay
recommended; Scottish Tourist Board five Crowns;
British Tourist Authority commended.
Open throughout the year.
Special breaks Winter breaks are available.
Price for dinner, with wine, bed and breakfast –
over £150.
Credit cards Access, Visa, Amex, Diners.
*The hotel has stairs everywhere so is not suitable for
disabled visitors.*
Overall mark out of ten 9

The very name Culloden evokes so many colourful images of
Scotland's tragic history that it would be a bitter disappointment

if Culloden House did not have an outstanding historical pedigree. As it happens, this imposing Georgian mansion was originally built as a Jacobean castle, and served briefly as the headquarters for the Young Pretender, Bonnie Prince Charlie, in the early eighteenth century, as he continued his ultimately hopeless quest to reclaim the Scottish throne. The surrounding land is Culloden Moor – the very ground where so much Scottish blood was shed and where the young prince made his last great stand in 1746 before fleeing to France to spend the rest of his life in exile. The actual battlesite is now in the care of the National Trust for Scotland, and the small headstones which mark individual clan graves are a poignant sight.

Culloden House itself was partly destroyed by fire later in the eighteenth century, and subsequently remodelled and rebuilt as a traditional-style Georgian mansion. It had a relatively undistinguished past from then until 1981 when the present owners, Ian and Marjory McKenzie, took over, promising to restore it to something approaching its former glory. The traditional Scottish feel to Culloden House is particularly appreciated by American visitors, and a staggering seventy per cent of those who stay at the hotel come from the United States.

Culloden House retains much of the 'old world' elegance which generations of earlier visitors would have known. Surrounded by forty acres of private parkland and majestic forest, the hotel is a particularly attractive example of Georgian architecture in this part of northern Scotland. Its central three-storey block is flanked by two further two-storey wings which are all interconnected by covered period passageways. A large lawn in front of the house is a popular site for wedding marquees; indeed, Culloden House is one of the favoured hotels in the Highlands in which to hold a society wedding reception. The lawn also doubles as a helicopter pad should guests choose to arrive in that manner.

The hotel's numerous public rooms, including a billiard room, retain a striking Georgian atmosphere, and subtle lighting enhances the elegant antique furnishings and writing tables which sit alongside deep armchairs for that relaxing after-dinner coffee. The house has a good collection of antique books which

31

are not chained or caged in, but freely available for residents to read. In eight years of running the hotel, Ian McKenzie says not one has ever been stolen. Conference facilities are particularly good at Culloden House and director-level and senior management meetings are encouraged by the resident proprietors.

Culloden House's most appealing public room *has* to be its restaurant. With seating for forty-five, it is decorated in traditional Adam style, and is reputed to be an authentic Adam design, although documentary evidence cannot be traced to prove this. The decor is dark green with white plaster relief and medallions – very elegant, and a more romantic setting than this room, when set and candle-lit at night, is hard to find.

Chef Michael Simpson serves a wide range of food in a combination of classical, *nouvelle cuisine* and Scottish Country House styles, and Ian McKenzie himself, resplendent in his traditional kilted Highland dress, presides over dinner each evening. Predominantly local produce is used in the preparation of all meals, and prime Scottish beef and fresh seafood are central features of the menu. An interesting speciality which was highlighted by *Gourmet* magazine was their (very fresh) locally caught Smoked Salmon served with an original Broccoli and 'Red Bell Pepper' which the chef makes with purple cauliflower and serves chilled with a dressing enhanced by a little finely chopped green chilli pepper. A very detailed wine list is also available.

The hotel has a total of twenty-one bedrooms, including one large family room and a four-poster. All have private bathroom facilities, colour television and direct-dial telephone. Leisure facilities available at Culloden House include a hard tennis court, sauna and billiard room. Nearby attractions include the Culloden battlefield; Loch Ness; Clava Cairns (best described as a mini-Stonehenge complete with Neolithic burial chambers); Cawdor Castle with strong Macbeth connections, and the town of Inverness.

11

GLEDDOCH HOUSE

Address Langbank, Renfrewshire PA14 6YE
Tel: 0475 54711 Fax: 0475 54201

Nearest town Glasgow.
Directions From Glasgow, follow the M8 towards
Paisley and turn off when you see the sign for
Langbank and Houston. Follow the B789 and signs
to the hotel.
Awards AA *** graded and rosette; British Tourist
Authority commended; Taste of Britain national food
award – Scottish outright winner; Scottish Tourist
Board four Crowns.
Open throughout the year.
Special weekend breaks are available throughout
the year.
Price for dinner, with wine, bed and breakfast for
two – over £150.
Credit cards Access, Visa, Amex, Diners.
*Children and dogs are allowed. The hotel is suitable for
disabled persons.*
Overall mark out of ten 8

Gleddoch House enjoys the distinction of being the youngest

Scottish Country House Hotel included in this guide. Built just sixty-four years ago, in 1927, by the great Scottish shipbuilder Sir James Lithgow, the house has retained strong links with the shipbuilding industry ever since. It was sensibly situated in 250 acres of idyllic west-coast countryside, enjoying some truly splendid views across the River Clyde estuary and the hills surrounding Loch Lomond. A small advantage of the hotel's location is the fact that just ten minutes will take you to or from Glasgow Airport.

The hotel has a total of thirty-three bedrooms, all of which are named after Scottish birds and each having individual characteristics. They vary considerably in size, and a number of the single rooms are a little on the small size. The hotel offers two types of single room: a standard single and an executive single which is specifically aimed at business visitors who might require extra space. These bedrooms have the attractive advantage of leather-inlaid writing desks, all well lit, and telephones that can be moved from their normal bedside-table location to the desk if you so desire. At the top of the range, there is an executive suite where up to eight people can be accommodated for a meeting if necessary.

All bedrooms are furnished to impeccable standards and include the luxuries you would expect in a hotel of Gleddoch's character including private bathroom facilities, colour television, tea and coffee making facilities and even four-poster beds if you feel like splashing out on that little extra.

The public rooms have obvious attractions to the business clientele, and this market is central to the hotel's trade. The large Garden Room offers unrestricted views across the terrace to the gardens and both lunch and dinner can be arranged here for up to forty guests. The house's original drawing room has a wide marble fireplace and richly ornate plasterwork all round, and accordingly makes a truly superior venue for a top-level business meeting where impressions are important.

Gleddoch House is blessed with an outstanding chef in Charles Price, and his bold promise to cook whatever dish you fancy (given a few days' notice) has yet to be beaten. Few residents, however, will want to stray far from his elegant à la carte menu which relies heavily on the best of local produce. Fresh Artichoke with Lobster, served warm on a bed of Spinach Noodles, is an extravagant opener (at over £10 per person) but easily the best hors d'oeuvre for what is to follow. But most wait for the main course before really spoiling themselves, and what better way to do so than by ordering Prime Aberdeen Angus Beef, or perhaps Breast of Partridge, served pan-fried with Woodland Mushrooms on a Truffle Essence, or maybe even Loin of Veal cooked with Stem Ginger and served with a Crisp Potato Cake bathed in a Cider Sauce. The menu prices are not cheap, even for a hotel of this calibre, so bear in mind a first-class meal for two, eating four courses and accompanied by a reasonable wine, is likely to leave you with little change from £90. The quality, presentation and surroundings, however, will be excellent.

Leisure facilities for the sportsman are plentiful at Gleddoch House. As a hotel guest, you will have access to some of south-western Scotland's finest golf courses and membership of the Gleddoch House Country Club where, in the Golf and Country Clubhouse, you will find a squash court, sauna facilities, plunge pool, international-size snooker table as well as the club lounge bar and restaurant. You can go horse riding from the hotel's own riding school without ever having to leave the spacious grounds.

Nearby attractions are almost too numerous to mention, but the most obvious attraction is the city of Glasgow itself just half an hour away by car. No more the dirty, run-down industrial city of the 1940s and '50s, Glasgow has undergone a major regeneration programme and is now a serious challenger for Edinburgh's crown as Scotland's cultural capital. Scotland's number one tourist attraction, the Burrell Collection, is twenty minutes away by car. To the north you have the breathtaking beauty of Loch Lomond and the Trossachs and, to the south, the Ayrshire coast. Further west, down the coast, are the yachting centres of Gourock and Inverkip.

12

GREYWALLS

Address Muirfield, Gullane, East Lothian EH31 2EG
Tel: 0620 842144 Fax: 0620 842241

Nearest town Gullane.
Directions From Edinburgh, follow the A198 to
Gullane. Greywalls is clearly signposted at the east
end of the town.
A member of the **Pride of Britain** consortium.
Awards Egon Ronay recommended.
Open from April until the end of October.
No **special breaks** are available.
Price for dinner, with wine, bed and breakfast for
two – over £150.
Credit cards Access, Visa, Amex, Diners.
*The hotel is suitable for disabled visitors and there are
ground-floor rooms; children and dogs are welcome.*
Overall mark out of ten 9

If you are a golf fanatic, or keen to find a peaceful retreat within
striking distance of Edinburgh, or just curious to look at the
small house which was once King Edward VII's bathroom, then
Greywalls is where you've been looking for. This tranquil
Country House Hotel was originally built in 1901 by one of

Britain's greatest Edwardian architects, Sir Edwin Lutyens, and considered a model mansion for its period even then.

The house's most famous guest was King Edward VII, who made regular visits here towards the end of his nine-year reign, between 1901 and 1910. Ostensibly the king came to relax and enjoy the views far across the Firth of Forth and the Lammermuir hills, but the real reason was his desire to visit Mrs Willy James, his mistress and wife of the house's owner. Such was the king's attraction to the house that they even built him a large private bathroom with a view across the garden! The two-room 'King's Loo' remains one of the hotel's most charming attractions, and is now a delightful bedroom, with en suite bathroom, overlooking the rose garden.

In 1924 the house was sold to Lt Colonel Sir James Horlick, grandfather of the present owner, Giles Weaver. It remained an upmarket holiday home until the Second World War when it saw service as an officer's mess for the RAF, and subsequently as a hospital for the Polish forces and their wives. Finally, in 1948, it was turned into a hotel and over the four decades which followed gradually improved and built up to the informal luxury standards you can expect today. Golf has been one of the central themes of life at Greywalls and its location at the very edge of the world-famous Muirfield golf course makes it an obvious favourite with golfers the world over. Many top professionals stay here during British Opens at Muirfield – and Tom Watson is known to have so loved the place that he's sneaked back a few times since.

The impressive hotel gardens were laid out by Sir Edwin Lutyens's imaginative friend and partner Gertrude Jekyll, and were lovingly tended for an incredible sixty years by the same gardener, James Walker. The house itself, garden walls, paths and hedges are all geometrically interlinked and plans are well in hand to recreate the small vegetable garden just as Mrs Jekyll had planned all those years ago.

Greywalls has a number of fine public rooms, but the panelled library is easily the most appealing and furnished in authentic period style right down to the last detail. On both sides of the big open fire there are shelves and shelves of books; ironically, many of the libraries in Country House Hotels today no longer have any books and have been converted into lounges instead. Refreshingly, the library at Greywalls still serves its original purpose. The Sunday papers, of all description, are laid out in the library and are an added treat to your huge Sabbath breakfast.

With seating for seventy, the dining room was once the court-yard of the house and now serves food in top modern English style. When it was constructed care was taken to ensure that Lutyens's original concept for the house's interior design was adhered to. Non-residents are welcome for dinner, but the management strongly urges advance booking, particularly during the month of August when the Edinburgh Festival is in full swing. The menu has a set price for four courses, with a small number of options and an additional charge if you wish to have a fifth course.

Paul Baron, the head chef, uses only fresh ingredients with which to create imaginative dishes and guests can choose between traditional menus and house specialities. A typical meal might consist of a starter of Pastry Tartlet with Crabmeat and Fresh Ginger, followed by a sorbet, then Mignons of Scottish Beef served in a red wine sauce with chopped shallot and thyme, finishing with Bitter Chocolate Torte. The wine list is extensive and well balanced, with bottles from under £10 to over £100. The quality of the cuisine is excellent.

The hotel has twenty-three bedrooms, five in a more modern extension and all furnished as closely to original period authenticity as possible and with their own private bathroom facilities. Most have views over the gardens or Muirfield golf course. When the house was first built there was a single bathroom so the renovations over the last few decades have made a tremendous improvement to the whole place.

Nearby attractions are obvious if you are a golfer: ten courses within a five-mile radius. A hard tennis court and croquet lawn are also available within the hotel grounds, but further afield you can visit Edinburgh and all that it has to offer, or the ancient castle of Tantallon, or the renowned bird sanctuary on the Bass Rock. Facilities for just walking and exploring are excellent and both the surrounding Lammermuir hills and the long sandy beaches nearby offer perfect opportunities for the inquisitive walker.

13

INVERLOCHY CASTLE

Address Torlundy, Fort William, Scotland PH33 6SN
Tel: 039770 2177 Fax: 039770 2953

Nearest town Fort William.
Directions Follow the A82 to Fort William and
continue on the same road for a further three miles
north. Inverlochy is located at the village of
Torlundy.

A member of the **Relais et Châteaux** consortium.
Awards AA **** (red) graded and two rosettes;
awarded Gold Plate Hotel of the Year award in 1971
by Egon Ronay; recommended (with rosette) by
Michelin guide. Awarded maximum five Red
Turrets by Michelin in 1986, the only Country
House Hotel outside London area to receive this
distinction.
Open from March until mid-November.
Price for dinner, with wine, bed and breakfast for
two – over £250.
Credit cards Access, Visa, Amex, Mastercharge.

Definitely one of Britain's top Country House Hotels, Inverlochy Castle is a romantic old Victorian building surrounded by a quite idyllic baronial estate. Queen Victoria herself spent a week here in 1873 and hit the nail firmly on the head when she wrote in her diaries: 'I never saw a lovelier or a more romantic spot.'

The castle was commissioned in 1863 by William Scarlett, third Baron Abinger and a former soldier, when he took the bold decision to sell the previous family seat of Abinger Hall in Surrey. By 1870 the first part of the new castle was complete and the family moved in, spending most of the year at their new home before returning to London for the winter. A huge staff was retained to look after Inverlochy Castle and its surrounding 39,000-acre estate throughout the year. Abinger retired from the army in 1877, fifteen years before his death, and became a local magistrate and much more actively involved in local affairs.

The castle remained in the Abinger family's possession until 1944 when it was sold to one Mr Hobbs of Vancouver, British Columbia. His family still own and run the hotel today, although it was as late as 1969 before the decision was taken to turn it into a luxury hotel.

Almost everything about Inverlochy Castle will amaze and, no doubt, impress you. A long elegant driveway, filled with well-tended shrubbery and floral displays and, in season, the rich smell of rhododendrons, makes for a welcome few hotels in Scotland can match. Inside the impression is no less striking. From the moment you enter the huge Great Hall, with its intricately decorated domed ceiling, you will be met by one of many smart, friendly and efficient staff who will make your stay here as smooth and trouble-free as possible. A staff of around fifty are on duty every day to look after a maximum of twenty-eight guests at any one time.

When you do enter the hotel, take a few moments to savour that first sight of this grand hallway, complete with authentic

41

crystal chandeliers, large oil paintings and a handsome carved wooden stairway which cascades down from the first floor. The high quality of the furnishings throughout the hotel befit the vast proportions of the public rooms, and accurately reflect the atmosphere of a former era.

The vast main public lounge is furnished in a style of timeless elegance rather than specifically Victorian or later. Every piece of furniture is of exceptional quality and the hotel's colour brochure can only struggle to do justice to any of the public rooms illustrated. Do look out for the billiard room, with its dark period table and traditional deer-antler wall hangings which quite complete the 'feel' of the place.

The main dining room has glorious views out across the nearby loch, and with a head chef trained and recruited from London's prestigious Connaught Hotel you are unlikely to be disappointed with the menu. The choice is not extensive, but the quality of food, standard of service and presentation are of the highest international standards. A couple of recommendations from the varied range of starters are Loch Linnhe Prawns in garlic and herb butter, and Paupiette of Smoked Salmon with a Dill and Mustard Sauce.

Main course specialities are always prepared from the finest local produce and include Poached Fillet of Baby Turbot with Vermouth Sauce and – a rarely seen main course option anywhere now – Roast Saddle of Hare with Juniper Berries. From their list of sweets, do watch out for the delicious Orange Soufflé – one of the chef's specialities. As you might expect from a hotel of this class, an extensive and balanced wine list is available.

The hotel has a total of sixteen bedrooms, of which most are extra large and all have an impeccable range of private facilities. A nice touch is the Strathmore mineral water and personalized soaps provided in all bedrooms. Room service is particularly comprehensive at Inverlochy.

Nearby attractions include the town of Fort William and Britain's highest peak, Ben Nevis; the West Highland Museum; a vitrified fort three miles up Glen Nevis; old fort walls behind Fort William's travel centre; Tor Castle (on the B8004 two miles

north-east of Banavie); and a wealth of sporting and outdoor
facilities within the hotel grounds, and in Fort William itself.

ISLE OF ERISKA

Address Ledaig, by Oban, Argyll PA37 1SD
Tel: 0631 72371

Nearest town Oban.
Directions From Oban, follow the A828 to Fort
William. The hotel is located four miles to the west,
at the mouth of Loch Creran, and is clearly
signposted.
Awards AA *** (red) graded; Egon Ronay
recommended; British Tourist Authority
commended; Scottish Tourist Board five Crowns –
very highly commended.
Open from March to November.
Special breaks Discounts for stays of seven nights
or more; advance reservations are only accepted
for a minimum of two nights.
Price for dinner, with wine, bed and breakfast for
two – over £150.
Credit cards Access, Visa, Amex and Diners.

Suitable for the disabled. Children are welcome and dogs are allowed if kept in bedrooms.
Overall mark out of ten 9

If you're seeking a truly private retreat, and at the same time want to be surrounded by the highest standards of traditional Country House comfort, then you should seriously consider a visit to the Isle of Eriska. This is a perfect honeymoon hotel and indeed, with the owner doubling as a Church of Scotland minister, you could even tie the knot while there and turn your visit into an unexpected honeymoon!

As its name suggests, the sandstone and granite hotel is situated on a 300-acre private island right in the middle of Loch Linnhe. A good road bridge is the sole connection with the mainland and the rest of civilization for however long you may choose to escape here. Much of the sprawling estate is left to mother nature's care so that guests can really enjoy the 'get-away-from-it-all' atmosphere to the full.

Enthusiastic proprietor Robin Buchanan-Smith has run the hotel since 1974 and his heavy personal and financial investments have long since begun to pay off. The house was built ninety years before his arrival in true Scottish baronial style for one of the Stewarts of Appin, a distant branch of the ancient Scottish Royal House of Stewart. The architect was really the last one of significance to flourish in Scotland before Robert Lorimer, and rejoiced in the name of Hippolyte Blanc. He was responsible for the Argyll Tower in Edinburgh Castle, probably his best-known commission.

The original owner died suddenly around the end of the last century while standing as a Unionist candidate in an Ulster election. Shortly afterwards his dubious business interests went bust and creditors came in to take over the house! The Clark Hutchison family eventually bought the house and lived here for a generation or so until circumstances caused its resale in 1930. Two sons, Sir Ian and Michael, entered Parliament for Scottish constituencies and still maintain contact with the hotel by visiting separately each summer, despite their advancing years.

The house fell into a state of neglect from 1930 until 1973, when the present owners took over and it took the Buchanan-Smiths over eight months, with a team of thirty workmen, to get the house smart enough to open as a Country House Hotel the following year. The results speak for themselves.

The various public rooms are spacious and elegant, typifying Victorian craftsmanship at its very best. Log fires are lit when the temperature outside demands it (which is quite often with Scotland's brisk west-coast breeze) and deep wall-panelling and rich plasterwork are delights to admire as you sit back, relax and enjoy your after-dinner coffee and home-made *petits fours* in the drawing room or the hall. Even the reception area is large and open with the emphasis on creating a warm and informal atmosphere. More than one guidebook has said that the personality of Robin Buchanan-Smith, a burly former university chaplain, quite dominates the hotel and this is certainly a fair assessment. He pledges that the island belongs to his guests and strives to make sure each visitor to Eriska will remember their stay long after the memory of most hotels would have worn off. He usually succeeds.

The dining room is decorated with pine panelling and a thick plaster-modelled ceiling. The emphasis is placed firmly on a traditional Scottish Country House style of cooking and presentation, under the expert eye of Robin's wife Sheena. Menus are changed nightly and nearly always include perfectly cooked fish as well as excellent sauces. Watch out for the Avocado Pears garnished with Crispy Bacon and Roasted Pine Kernels in an Olive Oil and Garlic Dressing as a starter. Roast Cushion of Veal carved at the table, glazed with Apricots served with a Cider and Apple Sauce makes an excellent main course choice. The helpings are generous and the food wholesome and simple with many of the vegetables and herbs coming straight from the walled garden. Breakfasts are a particularly lavish affair with every conceivable alternative from porridge, bacon and eggs and smoked haddock to snap, crackle and pop cereal. The freshly baked home-made bread, croissants and rolls prepared by Sheena Buchanan-Smith are reason enough to undertake the long drive from London. You might be disappointed if you come to Eriska expecting luxury continental cooking, but you will certainly not leave hungry.

Eriska has built its reputation on very high standards of comfort, faithful to the original Country House style rather than going overboard for pampered luxury. There is no sports complex, heated swimming pool or even a discreet sauna; indeed, leisure facilities are limited to gentle exploration of the 300-acre island and an assortment of watersports for the more energetic. All eighteen bedrooms have private bathroom facilities and include the standard extra of colour television.

Nearby attractions include the Isle of Iona, Glen Coe and surrounding countryside, and Inveraray Castle. If you can bring yourself – and have the energy – to leave the peace and tranquillity of the island, you can do anything from pottering around Oban and the islands to climbing nearby Ben Cruachan. Eriska also provides a warm and cosy retreat from the all too frequent mist and rain of the west coast. With a book or magazine from the eclectic selection in the library you need move no further than the blazing fire in the drawing-room. Finally, one of the more unusual 'guests' on the island is a badger who turns up regularly every night at the front door for his supper!

15

JOHNSTOUNBURN HOUSE

Address Humbie, near Edinburgh, East Lothian
EH36 5PL
Tel: 087533 696 Fax: 087533 626

Nearest town Edinburgh.
Directions Take A68 through Dalkeith and
Pathhead to Fala. Turn left on to B6457. After one
and a half miles, turn right at T junction.
Part of the **Mount Charlotte Thistle** hotel group.
Awards AA *** and Scottish Tourist Board four
Crowns – commended.
Open throughout the year.
Special breaks Details on application. Pheasant and
grouse shooting and clay pigeon shooting breaks by
arrangement. Special winter breaks are also
available.
Price for dinner, with wine, bed and breakfast for
two – over £150.
Credit cards Access, Visa, Amex and Diners.

Not suitable for the disabled.
Overall mark out of ten 7

Johnstounburn is a charming country retreat within easy driving distance of Edinburgh. It really is, as it claims, one of Scotland's most 'charming historic houses' – a turreted mansion house with all the classical features of an eighteenth-century estate – walled garden, parkland, outhouses – and it is now returning to its former splendour under the managership of the Mount Charlotte Thistle group.

Among its more interesting claims to fame is that in the 1950s the estate was owned by the uncle of John Hunt, one of the expedition which conquered Everest in 1953 with Sir Edmund Hillary. After the descent Hunt telegrammed Johnstounburn to let his family know the good news about the conquest, thus making Johnstounburn the first to know of the conquest before the news burst upon the rest of the world. It was also the home of the brewery baron, Andrew Usher, who was the first man in Scotland to blend whisky and start the new trend away from the traditional malts.

The main part of Johnstounburn was built in 1625, with the panelled dining room dating back to 1740. The house, as you see it today, was finished in 1840, with the most attractive stable conversions having been added in the last couple of years. Among the treasures of the house are two noteworthy mural paintings by the artist Robert Norie. However, the showpiece of this house stands outside in the gardens, the Dovecot, dating back to the eighteenth century and listed as a Historic Monument.

There are twenty bedrooms which have been completely refurbished. The recently converted stables, which are situated a five-minute walk from the main house, are particularly good for families or couples wishing a greater degree of privacy. They are more spacious, and give the occupants the benefit of having their own front door! The rooms in the house are more traditional, so if it's a romantic four-poster weekend you are looking for these would be more suitable. The hallmark of Johnstounburn is relaxation; the long history of the 'house as home' has been allowed to live on.

The food is described as French/Scottish. Certainly it features all the best Scottish specialities, such as prime Scotch beef, venison, game and seafood. The quality is first class, presentation good and service attentive without being fussy. The wine list is small but reasonably priced and particularly good value is the menu – still under £21 at the time of publishing. After a leisurely four-course meal which combines a delightful variety of tastes and colours, what better than to retire to the log fire in the lounge, for coffee and *petits fours*.

Nearby attractions are plentiful: the city of Edinburgh; the famous golf courses of East Lothian; fourteenth-century Tantallon Castle; bird-watching on the Bass Rock; Sir Walter Scott's home, Abbotsford; and Traquair House, the oldest inhabited house in Scotland.

16

KILDRUMMY CASTLE

Address By Alford, Aberdeenshire AB3 8RA
Tel: 09755 71288

Nearest town Huntly.
Directions From Aberdeen, follow the main A97
Ballater to Huntly road. Kildrummy Castle is
signposted.
A member of the **Best Western Hotels** consortium.
Awards AA *** RAC graded; Scottish Tourist Board
four Crowns – highly commended; British Tourist
Authority commended.
Open from mid-March until early January.
Special early/late season rates are offered for stays
of two nights or more.
Price for dinner, with wine, bed and breakfast for
two – over £150.
Credit cards All major cards.
*The hotel is unsuitable for disabled visitors; children and
dogs are welcome.*
Overall mark out of ten 8½

Kildrummy Castle is a little unusual in its origins, as it was deliberately *not* built on the site of, or even from the ruins of, a much older building. In fact, the present hotel dates only from 1900 when it was built as a private mansion house for Colonel James Ogston and it was inhabited as a family home right up to 1956 when it became a hotel. The origins of the first Kildrummy Castle go back a lot further, and the graceful ruins of the original thirteenth-century structure can be seen from the upper floor of the present hotel. Your first glimpse of them will be as you turn round a wide bend in the long rhododendron-lined driveway leading off from the main A97 up to the front of the hotel.

It is difficult to imagine the tall, roofless ruins of the old castle back in the days of its full glory, but it must truly have been an outstanding fortress when it was the family seat of the Earls of Mar, one of medieval Scotland's great noble families. It has lain abandoned now for centuries, but remains subtly looked after to ensure its timeless charm doesn't crumble away altogether, like so many of Scotland's ruined castles. The gardens at Kildrummy are outstanding: some time ago the National Trust for Scotland purchased the old estate grounds as well as the old castle. For a nominal sum you can enjoy these beautifully maintained grounds with their water features and varied tree species.

A strong feature of Kildrummy Castle is the proprietors' obvious intention to retain the intimate family house atmosphere as much as possible. The temptation to build on suites of new bedrooms has been resisted, although all sixteen bedrooms have been gradually upgraded to their present high standards. In addition to private bathroom facilities, all have colour television, direct-dial telephone, trouser press and tea and coffee making facilities as standard. Most of the bedrooms are comfortable without being remarkable, although a number of master doubles are available (and generally need to be booked further in advance). The master doubles represent excellent value and cost only a couple of pounds more per person – well worth the investment for that little bit extra space.

The hotel's public rooms are pleasing rather than luxurious with their period-style furnishings and oak panelling. The one truly outstanding public area is the main reception/hallway, with its criss-cross wood-panelled ceiling and superb Edwardian stair-case. The dining room, which is all non-smoking, is light and airy with seating for forty-two. Both à la carte and table d'hôte meals are available and there is a strong emphasis on local game produce, together with the fine traditional cuts of meat, fish and fresh produce which Aberdeenshire is rightly famous for.

The à la carte menu is impressive, containing seventeen main course options; you will not be disappointed with the Breast of Pheasant or Roast Country Chicken, gently cooked with a subtle Whisky Sauce. The restaurant's fish course options are varied, and include Grilled Scotch Salmon Maître d'hôtel, and a superb Poached Scotch Salmon served in a Mushroom, Chive and Whisky Sauce. The option of vegetarian dishes in the middle of the soup and fish options is an unusual addition to the menu, though no doubt a welcome one to vegetarians who will appreci-ate the fish courses. The accompanying wine list is comprehen-sive, containing a selection of over 120 different wines, including twenty-seven clarets. In addition, over thirty different half bottles are available from the wine list.

Nearby attractions are plentiful. For the golfer there are approximately thirty golf courses within an hour's drive of the hotel, and for the angler, three and a half miles of prime River Don on which to cast his rod. For the less energetic, no fewer than seven well-preserved castles and stately homes in the care of the National Trust for Scotland lie within easy reach – Fyvie, Craigievar, Castle Fraser, Leith Hall, Haddo House, Drum Castle and Crathes Castle. The Royal Family's official Scottish residence, Balmoral Castle, is approximately thirty minutes' drive from Kildrummy and the gardens are open all summer, whenever the Family is not in residence.

17

KINNAIRD

Address Kinnaird Estate, nr Dunkeld, Perthshire
PH8 0LB
Tel: 079 682 440 Fax: 079 682 289

Nearest town Perth.
Directions From Perth, take the A9 north
(signposted Inverness) and travel fifteen miles to
Dunkeld. After Dunkeld village turn left at the B898
(signposted Dalguise). Follow for four miles, and
hotel on right.
Awards Remy Martin Scottish Field restaurant
award for Best Newcomer 1989; John Webber is a
Master Chef of Great Britain, as appointed by the
Master Chefs Institute, and a Master Craftsman of
the Craft Guild of Chefs.
Open All year except the month of February.
Credit Cards Amex, Visa, Access.
*The hotel has a suitable room for the disabled. Children
under twelve years are not allowed. Dogs to stay in hotel's
kennels.*

Price For dinner, with wine, bed and breakfast for
two – over £200.
Overall mark out of ten: 9

An outstanding newcomer to the Scottish Country House scene,
and a hotel which will doubtless be making its mark internationally very shortly. With John Webber, ex-Gidleigh Park and
Cliveden, as chef/manager, and a fabulous eighteenth-century
Grade II listed house, sumptuously decorated, it was hardly a
combination which could miss.

Kinnaird was originally built in 1770 as a hunting lodge, and
was owned by the Atholl Estates up until 1927. Then it was
purchased by Lady Ward, whose American daughter-in-law
Constance is today's owner and the initiator of the remarkable
renovations that have made it into one of the country's finest
hotels.

The views of the moors and River Tay, which provide guests
with excellent sporting potential, can be enjoyed from many
of the public rooms, including the impressive billiards room,
adorned with some prize catches from the Tay in the 1920s. This
is rolling Perthshire – Scotland at its best.

In each of the eight guest rooms, and in the ground-floor suite,
you will notice the attention to comfort and detail. Luxurious
toiletries; pristine bed linen; monstrously thick bathrobes; mineral water, books and magazines aplenty; and ornaments and
furniture that many houses would reserve for the public rooms.
The decor is extremely pleasing, and the quality of the fittings
and soft furnishings creates an opulent air.

The cuisine alone is worth a trip from London. As you sip
your pre-dinner drinks in the grand Cedar Room or the intimate
library, take time to linger over the possibilities offered by the
evening's Tasting Menu. In addition to the à la carte, John
Webber offers guests the opportunity for a degustation on an
impressive scale. The only proviso is that all the guests at your
table must opt for it, to avoid the difficulty of serving six courses
to one person and three to another. A sample Tasting Menu
could encompass Timbale of Carrot, Roast Tail of Monkfish,
Gallette of Wood Pigeon and Foie Gras, Sautéed Best End of

55

Lamb, cheeses, and Hot Mango Soufflé. The price is around £38 per person, and includes coffee, *petits fours* and mineral water, and service charges, as they say, are neither included nor expected. The wine list is one of the most impressive in the country, with everything from very reasonable wines around the £12 mark to vintages at well over £100 per bottle. The style of cuisine is best described as modern style using local produce and based on traditional French. Webber is, after all, a protégé of Anton Mosimann.

Exercise is needed after all this rich living, and the 9000-acre estate copes admirably. There is shooting, fishing and stalking, and sporting parties are well catered for with the hotel's own gun room, gun safe and kennels. Two all-weather tennis courts are within the estate, and the walking potential is excellent. A croquet lawn/bowling green is located on the south side of the house.

Nearby attractions include Scone Palace, the National Trust Hermitage Walks at Dunkeld, the town of Perth, and the resort of Pitlochry.

18

KNOCKINAAM LODGE

Address Portpatrick, Wigtownshire DG9 9AD
Tel: 077681 471 Fax: 077681 435

Nearest town Stranraer.
Directions From Glasgow take the A77 to Stranraer
and follow the signs to Portpatrick. The hotel is
located three miles to the south of Portpatrick.
A member of **Pride of Britain**.
Awards AA ** (red) graded and two rosettes;
recommended with two red turrets and red M by
Michelin guide; Scottish Tourist Board four Crowns;
Egon Ronay recommended.
Price for four-course dinner, bed and breakfast –
£100–£150.
Credit cards Access, Visa, Amex and Diners.
*The hotel is unsuitable for disabled visitors. Children and
dogs are welcome.*
Overall mark out of ten 8

The tranquillity and seclusion of Knockinaam are exemplified by its having been chosen by Sir Winston Churchill as a secret meeting place with General Eisenhower and their Chiefs of Staff during the Second World War. The site was originally favoured by Lady Blair for the construction of a holiday house in 1869, to which enlargements were made in 1901. These dates encompassed a period of some of the finest domestic architecture in Scotland during the period of Victorian prosperity. In 1971 the house was bought by its present owner, a French chef, M. Marcel Frichot, who converted it into a 'restaurant avec chambres' and soon established a reputation for the finest cooking in the south of Scotland, while his wife, Corinna, ensured that the accommodation, with all its modern comforts, fully complemented the standards of cuisine.

Knockinaam's thickly wooded glen, beside which the house nestles, lends a softness to the protective cliffs which shelter this favoured spot. The house itself is not particularly remarkable in architectural terms, but its interior is well done, and the setting superb.

Its thirty acres of grounds range from gracious gardens and wide lawns sweeping down from the front of the house, to a small, sandy beach sheltered by its own miniature rocky headlands. Beyond lies the ever-changing sea stretching to the distant Irish coastline. Of all nature's displays of beauty, few can compare with the extended sunsets of long Scottish summer evenings, as sea and sky slowly merge in a blaze of glory at the day's end.

Naturally, the hotel's ten bedrooms are en suite and all enjoy open views over gardens and sea. Three are described by the proprietors as standard. Such a modest term for such elegance tells much more about the owner's standards than it does about the rooms. The next three rooms are more appropriately classified as superior, and the four most spacious and luxurious are accorded the status of master bedrooms. The Country House atmosphere comes into its own on cool evenings with oak panelling, paintings and antiques glimmering in the light of blazing log fires against the muted background of elegant soft furnishings. No comfort is sacrificed for this aesthetic pleasure, since the building has full central heating.

Marcel Frichot specializes in dishes inspired by fresh local produce such as beef from the world-renowned Galloway breed of cattle, named after this very area where the mild climate provides juicy grazing throughout the year, giving their meat all the goodness and taste that nature intended; or morsels direct from the sea in the forms of lobsters, scallops and scampi. These delicacies are always accompanied by home-grown vegetables and followed by local fruit and cheeses. Diners may recall the number of trucks they have passed on the road carrying this natural bounty to destinations in the south where no amount of expertise can restore the original freshness of taste. All the food at Knockinaam is prepared with the traditional skill and innovative imagination of a committed perfectionist.

Nearby attractions include the picturesque village of Portpatrick with its colourful crescent of houses around the little harbour, formerly a stepping-off point for Ireland. Its small fishing boats and pleasure craft provide a tranquil view for the relaxing holiday-maker, but reality is underlined by the town's lifeboat whose modest size belies its heroic reputation. To the northeast is Stranraer, ferry port for Ireland, prosperous agricultural market town and former county town with a fine range of attractive shops. At Whithorn in the south-east are the historic sites associated with St Ninian's early Christian mission to the pagan Britons.

19

MURRAYSHALL

Address Scone, Perthshire, PH2 7PH
Tel: 0738 51171 Fax: 0738 52595

Nearest town Perth.
Directions Murrayshall lies one mile north of Perth
on the A94.
Awards 1988 'Taste of Scotland' Restaurant of the
Year; 1989 Scottish Chef of the Year; Scottish Tourist
Board five Crowns – highly commended.
Open throughout the year.
Special Breaks Several different options available
throughout the year.
Price For dinner, with wine, bed and breakfast for
two – £100–£150.
Credit Cards Access, Visa, Amex and Diners
Children and dogs welcome
Overall mark out of ten 8½

Murrayshall Country House Hotel, Restaurant and Golf Course
is a tranquil, baronial style mansion situated close to Perth in
the heart of Scotland. Crow-stepped gables, steeply pitched

roofs and the occasional turret convey a solidity of architectural style typical of its Victorian origins.

The building was extensively refurbished and modernized in 1987: the previous austereness of its interior was then eradicated by the introduction of elegant decor, fittings and fabrics during this updating process. Today, the hotel marries antique furnishings with twentieth-century comfort and luxury. All of Murrayshall's sixteen bedrooms and three suites have en suite facilities, direct-dial telephone and colour television, while most of the bedrooms boast magnificent views over the hotel's 300–acre estate. The latter completely surrounds the hotel and offers an undulating vista of trees and open parkland, while nearer the house lies the productive walled kitchen garden.

A nice touch for guests staying more than two nights is the chef's offer to provide their own choice of main course. As its name suggests, the Old Master's Restaurant is adorned with Dutch oil paintings. Not for nothing has Murrayshall recently gained the coveted award of 'Taste of Scotland' Restaurant of the Year and its head chef Bruce Sangster Scottish Chef of the Year award. Its cuisine – which is essentially modern French with a Scottish flavour – is unquestionably of the highest standard. Fresh vegetables and herbs from Murrayshall's walled garden are used in season, while local produce forms the basis of most dishes. A dinner in the restaurant is a memorable experience: complementing the fine food and furnishings, you have the added pleasure of listening to a local musician, often playing classical music on a traditional instrument such as the Celtic harp.

Although menus are changed periodically, a typical starter might comprise Warm Salad of Starling Breasts, Quails Eggs and Back Bacon presented on a bed of Continental Leaves; or Chilled Roulade of Smoked Wild Tay Salmon and Turbot Mousse with a Dill and Mustard Sauce. This might be followed by Biquetou of French Goats Cheese gently grilled then presented bordered with a Salad of Garden and Continental Leaves, tossed in Walnut Oil with Toasted Pine Nuts; or what is intriguingly described as an 'Unusual Soup of Oban Mussels, served in a Vegetable Broth Perfumed with Saffron'. Main course dishes are no less spectacular. Medallion of Prime Scottish Venison with a Cassis and Redcurrant Sauce, or Fillet of Aberdeen Angus cooked in Butter with Oyster Mushrooms in its own Madeira Juices are just two of the 'French-Scottish-nouvelle' style dishes so well executed at Murrayshall.

As well as its exemplary cuisine, sporting facilities feature highly on the list of attractions here. The royal and ancient sport of golf is well represented at Murrayshall. Guests staying between October and March are offered a free round on the course, while the nominal fee of £10 a round is charged during high season. The eighteen-hole golf course has a well-appointed club house and Golf Society Room. Golf buggies and clubs can be hired, while a resident professional is on hand to tutor the novice or iron out faults in the more experienced player's game. Once you have mastered the hotel's own course you can enjoy some of the many other, world-famous golfing meccas to be found nearby. St. Andrews, for example, is only thirty-five minutes away, while Gleneagles is a mere nineteen miles distant.

For those who enjoy fishing and shooting, Murrayshall is an ideal base: deer stalking, fishing, clay pigeon and game shooting are all available locally, along with the hire of gillies and transport. Other sports for which facilities are available include archery, bowls, tennis and croquet. The surrounding area offers an abundance of attractions, from distilleries to glassmaking, palaces and castles to theatre. One individual touch offered by Murrayshall is a number of special day or weekend events. For example, if you want to refine your culinary talent, you can choose either a day's cookery course, or, for more serious gourmet devotees, a weekend masterclass, both supervised by Master Chef Bruce Sangster. Three- and four-day special breaks over Christmas and New Year give you the chance to keep the winter chill at bay, while enjoying the elegance of Murrayshall's superb surroundings and the excellence of its cuisine.

20

PITTODRIE HOUSE

Address Pitcople, Aberdeenshire AB5 9HS
Tel: 04676 444 Fax: 04676 648

Nearest town Inverurie.
Directions From Aberdeen, follow the A96
Inverness road. Once through the town of
Inverurie take the first road off to the left signposted
'Chapel of Garioch'. The village bearing that name
is about two miles down the narrow road, and the
hotel is signposted through the village.
Belongs to the **Scotland Heritage** group of privately
owned hotels.
Awards British Tourist Authority commended.
Open throughout the year.
Special breaks Winter breaks are available for at
least two nights, dinner, bed and breakfast.
Price for dinner, with wine, bed and breakfast for
two – £100–£150.
Credit cards Access, Visa, Amex and Diners.
Both children and dogs are welcome, but the hotel is

unsuitable for disabled guests unable to manage one flight of stairs.
Overall mark out of ten 7

The Pittodrie House Hotel is situated at the heart of a huge fertile 3000-acre Highland estate which comprises mixed arable, forestry and hill land. Surrounding the building is a three-acre walled ornamental garden which is at the disposal of residents to explore and enjoy. The hotel itself has a long history, dating back as far as 1480. Sadly, though, there is little remaining of the original medieval building, which was burnt to the ground by the Marquis of Montrose in the mid-seventeenth century. The Marquis did not have long to gloat on his triumph, however, as he was executed for high treason in 1650 during the Interregnum period.

The main ivy-covered hotel building which you can see today is a Z-plan castle which was rebuilt in 1675. Substantial Victorian improvements were made in the middle of the last century under the watchful eye of Aberdeen architect Archibald Simpson. The house remained in the possession of the Erskine family, a branch of the Earl of Mar's family, until the turn of this century, when the grandfather of the present owner bought it. Many of the original paintings and antiques from this time, and before, have been retained in the public rooms, and a few of the bedrooms.

The library, and main dining room particularly, have achieved an Edwardian atmosphere, with solid mahogany furniture, enormous original paintings (many of which have hung on these walls for over a century), large open fires and, of course, the beautiful views far across the surrounding grounds and distant hills which have pleased generations of visitors and residents alike. The library is occasionally used for private dinner parties for up to sixteen guests, and the subtle smell of antique books is a gentle reminder of the age of the hotel.

Wherever you choose to eat, it is unlikely that you will be disappointed by the quality of food served. The style is a combination of classical French and traditional Scottish, with emphasis on using only fresh local produce. The two-roomed restaurant seats up to seventy persons and, as tables are always kept available for residents, weekend booking for non-resident diners is essential. For occasional functions and large-scale dinners, the ballroom seats up to 150 guests.

The menu is limited but changes daily and the chef specializes in game and salmon dishes. For openers, a typical menu would include the choice of Haggis with Whisky Cream Sauce, or Smoked Woodpigeon Bagration. If you wish to have a soup and/or fish course there is no choice, and the option can be fairly unimaginative: Celery, Apple and Walnut Soup, for example, followed by Poached Plaice with Mussel Sauce. For your main course, though, the range is better and you may care to try out the marvellous Roast Haunch of Roe Deer with Cassis Sauce or the top speciality, Baked Darne of Salmon Maître d'hôtel.

Although Pittodrie House has twenty-seven double bedrooms, advance booking is strongly recommended. All have private bathroom facilities, television, telephone and so forth – and more often than not there is an extra piece of furniture in your room that will remind you that not all that long ago the hotel was still an elegant private home. Perhaps a piano, or an antique writing desk, or even a Victorian children's toy chest: you never can tell, but whatever the 'extra' happens to be, it is a lovely touch.

Leisure and recreation facilities at Pittodrie House are excellent. In addition to a billiard room, with international-size snooker table, there are two squash courts, a tennis court, and facilities for table tennis, croquet, clay pigeon shooting and endless possibilities for long, rambling hill walks from the hotel grounds. Horse riding and eighteen-hole golf can be easily arranged nearby.

Other nearby attractions for the less energetically inclined include the cities of Aberdeen and Inverness; the National Trust for Scotland's famous Castle Trail, which includes seven of Scotland's most famous castles and houses; Braemar; and Balmoral Castle, during the summer months when the Royal Family is not in residence.

21

ROMAN CAMP

Address Callander, Perthshire FK17 8BG
Tel: 0877 30003

Nearest town Callander.
Directions Follow the A84 as far as Callander. Enter
the hotel drive directly from the A84 at the east
end of Callander Main Street at the hotel sign
between two pink cottages.
A member of the **Historic and Romantic** hotel group.
Awards Scottish Tourist Board four Crowns –
commended; Egon Ronay recommended.
Open All year.
Special breaks A variety of special breaks are on
offer, depending upon the season.
Price for dinner, with wine, bed and breakfast for
two – over £150
Credit cards All accepted.
*The hotel is particularly well suited for disabled visitors
with one ground-floor room specially adapted for the
physically handicapped. Children of all ages and dogs are
welcome.*
Overall mark out of ten 7½

Despite its name, the Roman Camp Hotel and Restaurant has nothing particularly Roman about it. The present house was, in fact, given its name from the conspicuous earthwork which you can clearly see across the meadow to the south of the gardens. This is thought to be of Roman origin, and there is evidence of the site of a Roman fort at Bochcastle on the west side of the nearby town of Callander.

The house was built on the estate of the Earl of Mar, who was responsible for quite a number of the Scottish Country Houses included in this guide. Probably the Earl's best-known ancestor was the Regent of Scotland in the middle of the sixteenth century during the infancy of Mary, Queen of Scots.

The hotel's history is sketchy prior to 1897 when it is known that the house was acquired by the remarkable 2nd Viscount Esher, friend and confidant of several prime ministers and both King Edward VII and his son George V. In his time Esher became Governor of Windsor Castle and was the father of artist Dorothy Brett, perhaps best known for her 'Bloomsbury Set' friends, including Virginia Woolf and eventually D. H. Lawrence as well.

In his time, Lord Esher employed a team of Glasgow architects and had added considerably to the structure of the house by his later years. The present-day library, drawing room and the guest house, which is connected to the main building by a long passageway, were all his responsibility. The highlight of the walkway are the tapestries, which date from between 1937 and 1939, of English cathedrals.

The hotel's most striking public room is the ornate library which Lord Esher commissioned and so obviously loved towards the end of his long life. It has featured in a number of travel guides and press articles – particularly American ones – and has a curious 'lived-in' feel which many similar such hotel rooms lack. With its very ornate plaster ceiling, dark wood panelling, and shelf upon shelf of predominantly modern tomes, this room is a must for that informal morning coffee, or relaxed after-dinner liqueur, when you happily remember there is no need to rush home.

The other public room, apart from the spacious drawing room, is the dining room. It has a soft pink decor and a painted ceiling based on a traditional Scottish design, although the room is perhaps more suited to a business meeting than a romantic dinner. Advance booking, up to a week ahead, is essential for weekend dinner for non-residents.

Food concentrates on standard Scottish Country House style and the owner/chef, Sami Denzler, is a Swiss national who came to the hotel seven years ago, having previously owned and run his own restaurant in Edinburgh. As you might expect, the menu concentrates heavily on local game and fish, although Scotch beef and lamb feature most evenings as well.

The owner's Swiss origins mean that you can expect the rather odd spectacle of a fairly traditional Scottish menu written in French, with English translations underneath, a style of menu presentation usually reserved for more adventurous continental cuisine. A strong speciality is the chef's Filets de Sole aux Crevettes: Fillets of Sole with Shrimps in a White Wine Sauce. The extensive wine list contains a few pleasant surprises including one or two seldom seen Swiss and Australian bottles which are well worth trying.

When you're finally ready to call it a day you can retire to one of the hotel's fourteen bedrooms. Seven are on the ground floor and particularly suited to the elderly visitor. All rooms have private bathroom facilities, colour television and direct-dial telephone.

Nearby pursuits include endless possibilities for hill walking, golf and fishing. The hotel has its own stretch of the River Teith, which runs through the scenic, twenty-acre grounds. Private fishing is available for the exclusive use of guests. A number of obvious targets for sightseeing include Stirling, with its historic castle, Loch Lomond and the Trossachs, the site of the Battle of Bannockburn and Doune Motor Museum.

22

SHIELDHILL

Address Quothquan, Biggar, Lanarkshire ML12 6NA
Tel: 0899 20035 Fax: 0899 21092

Nearest town Biggar.
Directions From Edinburgh, take the A702 to Biggar
then the B7016 for two miles towards Carnwath.
At Shieldhill Road, turn left to the hotel, one and a
half miles distant.
Awards Scottish Hotel Guide Hotel of the Year 1990.
Open Closed from Christmas Day until New Year,
reopening on 4 January. Bed and breakfast only
from 4 January until 1 March.
Price For dinner, with wine, bed and breakfast for
two – £100–£150.
Credit cards All major credit cards accepted.
Overall mark out of ten 9

Shieldhill has stood amidst the rich farmland and undulating
hills of the upper Clyde valley since 1199. At that time it was a
Norman keep or small castle, stark, strategic and forbidding.
Shieldhill was sold by its then owners the Chancellor family in
1959 and turned into a hotel. More recently it was bought by

Christine Dunstan and Jack Greenwald, and today, several centuries after its military origins, Shieldhill now offers a homely, welcoming atmosphere within its luxuriously appointed interior. All this has happened by dint of much hard work and a considerable financial investment on the part of its owners.

Beyond the hotel building, its gardens, lawns and rolling woodland beckon you to wander and catch a glimpse of the varied wildlife within the grounds. The hotel's exterior is a mixture of architectural styles and periods. The 'Old Keep', with its turreted roof, secret stairway and priesthole, conveys an atmosphere of history and intrigue, and it's not difficult to believe that the reputed Lady in Grey, Shieldhill's (friendly) resident ghost, still inhabits the hotel.

Once inside the hotel itself, a wide hall leads to a welcoming, oak-panelled room, with open fire and always-fresh flowers. Several imaginative design themes run through the rooms of the building, one such being the presence of opulent, richly coloured carpets, commissioned especially, and bearing the Chancellor family crest throughout.

Each of the hotel's eleven bedrooms is named after a famous Scottish battle, such as Bannockburn, Glencoe and Otterburn. Every room, though individually and distinctively different, is held together by the common theme of Laura Ashley's Venetian collection of wallpaper and fabrics. Each bedroom has its own private bathroom, some with jacuzzis, while a number contain fireplaces, four-poster beds and antique furniture. 'The Chancellor', Shieldhill's honeymoon suite, boasts a king-size bed and a high, double jacuzzi, sunk into a thickly carpeted platform. Bedroom views are delightful to behold, either overlooking Shieldhill's lawns and woodland, or stretching beyond to the undulating Clydesdale hills.

The restaurant overlooks the parklands and attractive rustic scene of Shieldhill's working farm. Brian Graham is the hotel's reputable Chef de Cuisine. His style is essentially French, with a Scottish influence, and his excellent menu is changed at least twice a month. The food is of an exceptionally high standard, with choices such as Sliced Scottish Salmon with Summer Leaves and Lemon, and a half Charentais Melon and Strawberries glazed with Glayva Sabayon served with an assortment of Fresh Berries and Mandarin Sorbet as excellent appetizers. Mouthwatering intermediate-course options include such choices as Steamed Oban Mussels in White Wine and Cream and Fresh Garden Herbs, and Breast of Woodland Pigeon with Blackcurrant Essence and a Crispy Basket of Creamy Mushrooms. For one's main course, I recommend Grilled Fillet of Salmon topped with a Crabmeat and Ginger Crust on a Dill and Vegetable Beurre Blanc, though Steamed Supreme of Free Range Chicken filled with a Scallop Mousseline served on a Lime and Basil sauce is a worthy alternative. All main-course dishes are served with a selection of fresh market vegetables and potatoes. There is a good vegetarian choice on the menu – a refreshing change from many other Country House Hotels.

Although leisure facilities are restricted within the hotel grounds, there are four challenging golf courses within fifteen minutes' drive of Shieldhill. Salmon fishing on the River Tweed can be arranged, given sufficient warning, as can game shooting.

23

SUNLAWS HOUSE

Address Kelso, Roxburghshire ED5 8JZ
Tel: 05735 331 Fax: 05735 611

Nearest town Kelso.
Directions Sunlaws is situated three miles south-west of the town of Kelso on the main A698 Kelso to Jedburgh road at the south side of Heiton village. An independent hotel owned by the Duke of Roxburghe.
Awards AA *** graded; Egon Ronay 74%; Michelin two black turrets recommended; Scottish Hotel Guide (rosette for food)
Open throughout the year.
Special breaks A good variety are available throughout the year including Weekend breaks, While-Away breaks, and both Shooting and Fishing breaks.
Price for dinner, with wine, bed and breakfast for two – over £150.
Credit cards Access, Visa, Amex, Diners.
Facilities for disabled visitors are excellent, including

several ground-floor rooms and a specially adapted toilet;
children and dogs are both welcome.
Overall mark out of ten 7½

One of very few Country House Hotels in Great Britain which are still owned by a titled member of the aristocracy, Sunlaws is part of the estate of the Duke of Roxburghe, and can fairly claim to be one of the Border's top hotels. The present hotel is actually the third building which has been constructed on this site in the last two centuries, as a combination of fire, fair wear and tear and general expansion have taken their toll since then.

The hotel you can see today dates from the 1860s, but just over a century earlier, on 5 November 1745, it is reputed that Bonnie Prince Charlie stayed at the house which was then Sunlaws, and planted a white rose-bush somewhere in the surrounding grounds whilst the Jacobites were massing in Kelso before their march south. Then owners, the Scott-Kerr family, were known supporters of the Stuart cause, so the story is certain to contain some grain of truth. Two residents from former times are still said to haunt part of the house; one sad lady is reputed to walk the ground floor of the hotel, and an old soldier can still occasionally be heard on the turret battlements. Sightings are very rare, though, and pretty certain not to interrupt the enjoyment of your stay here.

Set in 200 acres of fine country estate, the hotel retains the feel of a converted country gentleman's retreat, offering much of the traditional comfort visitors in earlier generations would have known and appreciated. It is smartly furnished throughout and although the high standards of comfort offered are never in doubt, the choice of furnishings in some of the public rooms tends a little too much towards the modern.

However, this is a very small niggle and the very striking wood-panelled Library Bar more than compensates for this. As you sit by the roaring log fire, with its ornate Victorian fireplace, it is all too tempting to cast your mind back to the days when the local gentry used to meet here to discuss such weighty matters as where to head for their next fox-hunt, or even the vintage of the house port!

The restaurant seats some forty-five people, although for luncheon guests have the opportunity of dining in the Library Bar and so savouring its atmosphere that bit longer. On warm days, and there *are* a few during the early summer months, particularly in this part of Scotland, a fixed price Country Luncheon is also available in the large conservatory. Both are served from 12.30 p.m. until 2 p.m. throughout the week.

Under Head Chef Chris Webb, the cuisine is quintessentially Scottish Country House style, with the emphasis on local produce, as you might expect. The menu is changed daily. Non-residents (who generally make up about one-third of the clientele on any given evening) can enjoy dinner for around £25 a head – slightly more if you add a modest wine from the hotel's wine list.

The range of hors d'oeuvres is deceivingly adventurous if you look at it closely. Baked Fillets of Local Trout with a creative Orange and Cucumber Sauce; Chilled West Coast Oysters with Guinness; and even Eyemouth Langoustine Tails grilled with Garlic Butter are just three of the possibilities. From the main course options, East Coast Lobster and Scallops in a Cream and Drambuie Sauce, served with rice, are outstanding value at around £10 at the time of publication. Equally the chef's Grilled Angus Sirloin with Anchovy Butter is good value at a few pounds dearer, although the generous portions of vegetables will set you back another few pounds. One of the unusual features of Sunlaws is the selection of malt whiskies from the Library Bar. This selection contains several whiskies not commercially available, and others from now defunct distilleries.

Sunlaws House has a total of twenty-two bedrooms, including one well-appointed single, and all with private bathroom facilities. Most bedrooms are pleasantly spacious, although not all are to the generous extent of the blue-carpeted double featured on the hotel's advertising brochure. Six are located in the stable courtyard and all have colour television, radio alarm and direct-dial telephone.

Nearby attractions include Floors Castle, a magnificent stately home and private residence of the hotel's owner, the Duke of Roxburghe. Complimentary admission is available to hotel residents during the summer season. Other attractions include a range of leisure facilities like croquet, shooting, hard court tennis, salmon and trout fishing, and both golf and horse riding within the immediate area of the estate. For keen shooters, there is a resident shooting instructor based permanently at Sunlaws. More leisurely attractions include Abbotsford, former home of Sir Walter Scott, Bowhill, Mellerstain, Thirlestane Castle, and the magnificent collection of ancient abbeys at Dryburgh, Jedburgh, Melrose and Kelso itself. The city of Edinburgh is just over an hour's drive away with all that it offers visitors to Scotland.

For a rather unique experience, falconry breaks are a new addition to the range of pursuits offered at Sunlaws. These breaks are offered in conjunction with the Scottish Academy of Falconry.

Northern England

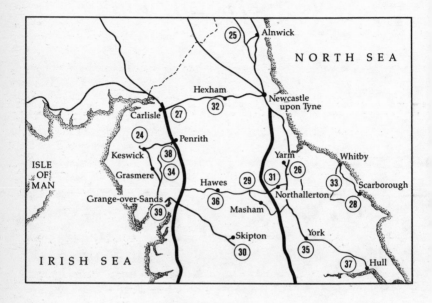

Northern England

24

ARMATHWAITE HALL

Address Bassenthwaite Lake, Keswick, Cumbria
CA12 4RE
Tel: 07687 76551 Fax: 07687 76220

Nearest town Keswick.
Directions From the M6, exit at junction 40
signposted Penrith. Follow the A66, bypassing
Keswick, and branch off on to the A591 (signposted
Carlisle) at the major roundabout. Travel for about
eight miles to a crossroads; turn left at the Castle
Inn Hotel for 200 yards.
Awards AA **** graded, Egon Ronay and Michelin
recommended.
Open throughout the year.
Special breaks Winter breaks available from the
beginning of November until the end of April,
excluding Bank Holidays; also special Christmas
and New Year programme.
Price for dinner, with wine, bed and breakfast for
two – over £150.
Credit cards Access, Visa, Amex and Diners.

The hotel has specially adapted rooms for the disabled; children and dogs are accepted.
Overall mark out of ten 9

Twenty miles from Carlisle, sitting by the edge of Bassenthwaite Lake, Armathwaite Hall is one of Cumbria's best hotels and one of the best-value upper-price-bracket Country House Hotels featured in this guide. As the proprietor states, Armathwaite Hall offers a type of holiday associated with English life at its best: good food, luxurious surroundings, and acres of natural beauty all around you.

Armathwaite Hall was built in the late eighteenth century, and was a grand country house even then. For centuries the original building on the site of the present house was home to a convent of Benedictine nuns, and although the convent was 'wretchedly poor' it was frequently plundered and finally dissolved during the Reformation.

The current house was purchased in 1796 by one Sir Frederick Fletcher Vane, and it remained the Vane family seat for generations. Prior to then the surrounding grounds and Bassenthwaite Lake had been the subject of considerable controversy when the Earl of Egremont and Sir Wilfred Lawson fought each other in the assize court of Carlisle for the rights to the area. It was swiftly decided that: 'The lake and every part thereof is of the freehold of the Earl of Egremont . . . and the said Earl and his tenants are entitled to the privilege of drawing and landing nets.'

Wherever you wander in the public areas of the hotel, you will appreciate it has been built to baronial proportions. The main lounge area has an enormous fireplace, usually set with a welcoming log fire, and is oak panelled all around. Antlers, pewter plates from earlier generations and soft lighting enhance the feeling that this really is one of northern England's most authentic Country House Hotels. The hotel's large wood-panelled restaurant can seat up to eighty people at any one time. The ceiling is one of the most intriguing features of the whole hotel, with its deep square-set octagonal pattern contrasting with the more modern furnishings. A huge wooden carved fireplace dominates the longer wall, opposite the large windows which look out across the lake.

Both an à la carte and a table d'hôte menu are available each evening; their popularity is reflected by the management's earnest request for bookings as far in advance as possible by non-residents. Several menus are available and the table d'hôte changes daily. The emphasis is on quality and the style is predominantly French. From the menu gourmande, Cassoulette d'Escargots à L'aneth makes a mouthwatering starter, and to follow, the magnificent double fillet steak Châteaubriand for two or the Délice de Volaille à la Homardine are recommended.

The hotel has forty-two bedrooms, including five studio suites – one with private tower and one with four-poster bed – all of which are extremely popular and require considerable advance booking. All rooms are a good size, and comfortably furnished. Standards are being improved all the time, but all have private bathroom facilities and colour television which includes an in-house video service.

Armathwaite Hall has an extensive range of leisure facilities to suit all tastes. The hotel's leisure club has an indoor heated swimming pool, sauna, solarium, spa bath and gymnasium and hairdressing and beauty salon. Other attractions include facilities for tennis, darts, golf, snooker and pitch and putt. A recently opened Equestrian Centre provides superb country hacks, while qualified instructors give lessons for all riding abilities, in the all-weather outdoor arena.

Nearby attractions are plentiful: Lingholm Gardens, near Keswick; Lowther Wildlife Adventure Park; Munchester Castle; Windermere Steamboat Museum; the town of Kendal, with its popular museum of natural history and archaeology; Dent Craft Centre; the Haverthwaite Railway, near Newby Bridge; the city of Carlisle; and the surrounding natural beauty of the Lake District as a whole.

25

BREAMISH HOUSE

Address Powburn, Alnwick, Northumbria NE66 4LL
Tel: 066 578 266 Fax: 066 578 500

Nearest town Alnwick
Directions The hotel is approximately thirty-eight
miles north of Newcastle-upon-Tyne, leaving the
A1 for the A697 Wooler to Coldstream road.
Awards AA ** (red) graded; Egon Ronay and
Michelin recommended; English Tourist Board four
Crowns.
Open from February until the end of December.
Special breaks Mini-breaks available from February
until April, and again from mid-October until 30
December.
Price for dinner, with wine, bed and breakfast for
two – £100–£150.
Credit cards None accepted.
*Only the restaurant is suitable for the disabled; children
under twelve not permitted, and dogs by arrangement in
advance.*
Overall mark out of ten 8

Set amid five acres of gardens and woodland on the edge of a national park, Breamish House has an extremely peaceful rustic setting which understandably attracts dozens of repeat visitors each year. The hotel was built in the seventeenth century, and was originally a large farmhouse. In the nineteenth century it was extended to become a Georgian-style hunting lodge and, this century, converted from a private home into a small luxury hotel.

The resident proprietors have striven hard to achieve a balance of comfort and period charm. They pride themselves on a friendly and caring service, where it is possible to relax and feel at home from the moment you arrive at the hotel. From the exterior, the hotel looks rather unspectacular; it is a standard-design Georgian house, with symmetrical stonework and ident-ical rectangular windows. Inside, though, the house has been furnished in the style of the period when it was a private resi-dence, but it would be fair to say the emphasis is more on informal comfort than pampered luxury.

Two main public rooms, a sitting room and a drawing room, offer excellent views across the surrounding Northumbrian countryside. It might be worth bearing in mind if you smoke that the dining room is strictly non-smoking.

Breamish House is recognized as one of the best small hotels in Northumberland, and its bright public rooms and quality of cuisine justify this. The hotel has not attempted to enter the upper league of luxury Country House Hotels, and this is reflected in the fact that the AA have awarded Breamish two red stars, for outstanding quality within its given class, but just two stars nevertheless.

Breamish has ten bedrooms, all with private bathroom facili-ties, colour television and telephone, and a number of pleasing little touches like quality toiletries to make your stay that little bit more comfortable. The courteous staff are very attentive to small details, particularly where culinary preferences are con-cerned. Indeed, this attention to detail was one of the principal attractions highlighted by the Consumers' Association in their write-up of this hotel in their guide.

The dining room is wonderfully informal. Your typical day

begins with a hearty Northumberland breakfast, which can include the famous locally smoked kippers, but is guaranteed to give you a good start whatever you have planned for the rest of the day. A wonderful 'traditional' Sunday lunch is available each weekend. In the evening, though, whatever day of the week it is, dinner is selected from a standard price table d'hôte menu – excellent value at around £15 per person at the time of publication. The choice is limited to around three or four dishes for each course, but the presentation and quality of food is excellent. Popular starters include Mushrooms marinated with Red and Green Peppers, or an interesting cocktail of Melon, Grapes and Pineapple in Vinaigrette Dressing. A home-made soup, which is generally a chef's favourite, like Cream of Parsnip or Cauliflower follows before the main course – which usually contains at least one fish choice from locally caught produce. Non-fish specialities include Roast Loin of Lamb with a Purée of Onion, Thyme and Celery, served with stuffing and mint salad; or perhaps Fillet of Pork cooked with fresh Marjoram, Parsley, Rosemary and Garlic, served with the succulent pan juices and glazed oranges.

Leisure facilities at Breamish House are rather limited, although all the usual outdoor sporting activities – golf, fishing, horse riding, hillwalking and so forth – can be arranged nearby. The hotel lies at the foot of the Cheviot hills, and the Coquet and Ingram valleys lie nearby. To the east lies the dramatic and secluded Northumbrian coastline, perfect for long walks and gentle exploration. Nearby attractions include Holy Island and the Farne Islands bird sanctuary, as well as Floors Castle (stately home of the Duke of Roxburghe), and the Border towns of Kelso, Hawick and Selkirk with the countless attractions they have to offer the visitor to this region.

26

CRATHORNE HALL

Address Crathorne, Yarm, Cleveland TS15 0AR
Tel: 0642 700398

Nearest town Yarm.
Directions Crathorne Hall is close to the A19 trunk
road on the way from Thirsk to Yarm; follow the
signs to Crathorne village.
Part of **Voyager Hotels Ltd**.
Awards AA **** graded; Egon Ronay grade 1 hotel;
Michelin recommended.
Open throughout the year.
Special breaks Weekend breaks are available; theme
breaks are offered from time to time.
Price for dinner, with wine, bed and breakfast for
two – £100–£150.
Credit cards All major cards accepted.
*The hotel is unsuitable for the disabled; children and dogs
are allowed.*
Overall mark out of ten 8

Crathorne Hall has the distinction of being the largest Country

House built during the nine-year reign of Edward VII, which lasted from 1901 until 1910. The hotel is set amid fifteen acres of rolling green countryside, just by the little Yorkshire village of Crathorne. Just as in the days when the hotel was first built, visitors can appreciate its prime location right above the Leven Valley, with wide panoramic views to the Cleveland hills beyond.

The interior of the house has lost little of its Edwardian style and elegance. The huge drawing room is one of two spacious public lounges, and contains a number of impressive oil paintings dating back to the era when the house was built, and before. The room is dominated by an enormous wood-carved coat of arms mounted above the fireplace, and is furnished with a combination of period furniture and comfortable modern armchairs which blend well with the Edwardian feel of the room.

The hotel is a popular venue for business seminars, conferences, society functions, weddings and so forth, and on these occasions the large ballroom, with its great views across the Leven Valley, is used. For particularly grand functions the drawing room, ballroom and dining room all interconnect, providing a most impressive setting which allows up to 200 people to be accommodated in style at any one time.

The dining room is another magnificent old room, its size and enormous stone fireplace typical of Edwardian lavishness in the decade or so prior to the outbreak of the First World War. Half-wall wood panelling goes all the way around the room, adding to the 'warm' feel. Cast your eyes heavenwards for a few moments while you are waiting for your meal to be served and enjoy the elaborately decorated ceiling, its raised square pattern marked out in rich gold leaf against a brilliant white background.

Despite its size, the restaurant offers a surprisingly intimate atmosphere. The chairs are comfortable and of modern design, crafted in an uncomplicated fashion which will not detract from the splendour of the room around you. Food is served in a French style, although some of the best features of English cooking (such as the traditional Sunday lunch) have not been forgotten. Local game specialities are particularly popular during the appropriate season, and the restaurant is as popular with non-residents as it is with residents throughout the year. Advance booking, particularly at weekends, is essential.

Crathorne Hall has a total of thirty-nine bedrooms, and each room is unique in style and design. Much of the original Edwardian charm remains: the ornate friezes where the walls meet the ceiling, pieces of antique furniture, long flowing curtains and so on. Each room has a limited edition graphic print on its walls and, in addition, all bedrooms have their own private facilities. Each one has been fitted with the sort of modern comforts you would expect in a quality hotel like this, such as colour television, telephone, and an assortment of complimentary toiletries. All rooms have large windows and splendid views across the grounds and surrounding countryside.

At the time of writing this Grade II listed building was to have another wing added to balance the present, slightly lopsided look, using carefully blended stone. The orangery will become an indoor swimming pool and the elegant stables an open-air restaurant.

Apart from swimming and tennis, Crathorne Hall has no designated sporting areas, but most popular sporting facilities, including golf, fishing and shooting, can be arranged locally. Nearby attractions include Leven Valley and the Cleveland hills beyond, the coastal towns of Whitby and Hartlepool, and the city of Newcastle within an afternoon's drive.

27

CROSBY LODGE

Address Crosby-on-Eden, Cumbria CA6 4QZ
Tel: 0228 73618

Nearest town Carlisle.
Directions Leave the M6 at junction 44 – the last
junction on the motorway, or first if travelling from
Scotland. Follow the B6264 and you will soon see
the hotel signs.
Awards AA *** graded; British Tourist Authority
commended; English Tourist Board four Crowns;
Egon Ronay and Michelin recommended.
Open late January until Christmas Eve.
Weekend breaks are available from October until
the end of March.
Price for dinner, with wine, bed and breakfast for
two – £100–£150.
Credit cards Visa, Amex.
The hotel is unsuitable for disabled guests; children and
dogs accepted by prior arrangement.
Overall mark out of ten 7½

Just a few miles into England from the Scottish border, Crosby

Lodge is an extremely popular stop-over point for businessmen and tourists alike travelling either north or south on the busy M6 motorway. Even so, the hotel has a wonderfully secluded location which also makes it popular for couples looking for that informal romantic hideaway to enjoy a second (or even a first) honeymoon, or just a special weekend.

The Lodge is a converted country mansion, originally built at the beginning of the nineteenth century by a wealthy local magnate. It was a private residence until 1969, although was allowed to run down considerably during the earlier part of this century. Present owners Michael and Patricia Sedgwick bought the house in 1970, and after an extensive programme of renovation and redecoration finally opened the Lodge as a Country House Hotel in 1971.

Crosby Lodge sits in a beautiful pastoral setting near the village of Low Crosby. Several acres of neatly tended gardens encircle the hotel, and a particularly well looked-after walled garden is marvellously peaceful and the perfect place for a leisurely stroll before dinner or after a full Sunday lunch.

As far as possible, authentic antique furnishings have been retained throughout the hotel. Wherever you go inside Crosby Lodge you are likely to be struck by a feeling of space. All the public rooms, and the bedrooms, are large and airy, and the atmosphere is as informal as it is unhurried throughout your stay. The hotel is popular for weddings, anniversary and birthday parties, and can suit a wide range of business functions. The large Cocktail Bar is a popular local social spot, although the influx of non-residents at the weekend is seldom obtrusive.

The restaurant has an uncluttered feel, with more than enough space around each table and chair to allow resident and non-resident diners the opportunity to relax and enjoy their meal, and never will you get the sensation of being hurried along to finish your coffee and go. Michael Sedgwick himself takes charge of the kitchen, along with two assistant chefs and son James who joined him in 1987.

Crosby Lodge's menu is a successful mixture of traditional English and French cuisine, although it is increasingly drawing on *nouvelle cuisine*, with lightly cooked vegetables and herby sauces. All the baking is done on the premises, including home-made scones, biscuits and *petits fours*, while all your morning jams and marmalades come from the kitchen here.

A table d'hôte and an à la carte dinner menu are available each evening, with a most impressive range of starters which clearly gives away Michael Sedgwick's area of culinary special-ity. There is an emphasis on fish-based dishes, and two succu-lent treats really stand out: Grilled Large King Prawns with a Mild Garlic Dip, and Prawns Thermidor, served in a Cream Sauce with Wine, Mushrooms and Cheese. Both are exquisite.

There are eleven bedrooms, including one family room and one single, which have all been individually designed and fur-nished to very high standards of comfort. En suite bathroom, direct-dial telephone, colour television and hairdryer come as standard. Most have superb views of the surrounding grounds, and a number have massive antique half-tester beds. These are almost always more comfortable than standard doubles, to say nothing of being at least a foot higher off the ground, and if you are coming to Crosby Lodge for that special romantic break, it would be a sensible idea to reserve a half-tester room when you book.

Crosby Lodge has nothing to speak of in the way of leisure facilities, other than an extensive range of walks and strolls around the spacious grounds. Nearby attractions include the city of Carlisle, with its imposing castle and famous cathedral (said to be one of the smallest in the world); the beautiful Gallo-way coast, or Scottish Borders, only an hour or so away by car; the city of Edinburgh, an excellent day trip if you have never visited Scotland; and, of course, the breathtaking Lake District all around you in Cumbria.

28

HACKNESS GRANGE

Address North Yorkshire Moors National Park,
near Scarborough YO13 0JW
Tel: 0723 882345 Fax: 0723 882391

Nearest town Scarborough.
Directions Follow the A64 from York and turn left
at Staxton roundabout. Continue until Seamer,
taking first left at roundabout there to village of
Ayton. Just past a garage on the left there is a
sharp right turn to Firge Valley and Hackness. Four
miles along this road turn left at T-junction and
the hotel is 400 yards down this road in the village
of Hackness.
A member of the **Best Western Hotels** consortium.
Awards AA *** graded; Ashley Courtenay
recommended.
Open throughout the year.
Details of **special breaks** available on request from
the hotel.
Price for dinner, with wine, bed and breakfast for
two – £100–£150.

Credit cards All major cards accepted.
The hotel is suitable for the disabled; childen are allowed,
but dogs are not permitted.
Overall mark out of ten 7

The most exceptional feature of this delightful Country House
Hotel is its location. Hackness Grange is located in the picturesque Yorkshire village of Hackness, six miles inland in the
North Yorkshire Moors. The hotel itself stands in eleven acres
of private grounds on the banks of the River Derwent, enjoying
fine views across the surrounding countryside, and is popular
with nature lovers and city-dwelling guests alike.

Hackness Grange was built near the beginning of the nineteenth century, and in 1890 the property was enlarged to be
occupied by the second Lord Derwent, and subsequently by the
Earl of Listowel. Extensive modernization has taken place over
the last decade or so, and the result has sadly meant that much
of the Victorian charm of the place has been lost in concessions
to modern comfort: plush wallpaper where wood panelling
would have looked more in keeping, and so forth.

All the public rooms have blazing log fires during the winter
months, adding to the warmth and enthusiasm with which the
hotel staff will greet you. Throughout your stay, the management work hard to develop a house-party kind of atmosphere,
something which naturally relies very much on the cooperation
of the residents, but on the whole the atmosphere is convivial,
relaxed and informal.

There are twenty-six bedrooms, all with en suite bathroom
facilities, refrigerated minibars, colour television and so on. A
number of rooms are a little lacking in character, and although
all are individually styled, one or two of the twin rooms are
fitted with rather modest-quality furnishings. A programme of
refurbishment is, however, planned. One positive point about
bedroom facilities is the nine ground-floor bedrooms available,
in the Courtyard Wing, which are ideal for disabled visitors.

Hackness Grange has a bright Regency-style dining room,
offering good views across the hotel lake and surrounding
valley. The brown and gold striped decor is a little overpower-

ing, but the thick drapes around the wide bay windows do neutralize the effect considerably. A full silver service is on offer, and a reasonable wine list complements the table d'hôte menu which offers four or five choices for each course nightly.

The menu restricts itself to traditional English cooking. Dishes are filling and wholesome, with few culinary surprises but at least three or four choices per course. Cheese and Pear Salad or Mushroom and Ham Pancakes are among the more original starters available. A sorbet or modest salad-style intermediate course follows, and that may include something like Poached Fillet of Plaice or similar. Lamb, pork and sirloin steak all feature as main dishes and seafood vol-au-vents, more commonly seen as a starter, are occasionally available as a main dish. One luxury which shouldn't be missed, if possible, is the delicious Fresh Strawberry Pavlova to round off your meal. This dish is extremely popular, and positively overflows with fresh straw-berries and cream – it is even available when strawberries are out of season.

The hotel has a small indoor heated swimming pool, and other leisure facilities include a nine-hole golf course, a pitch and putt area, croquet lawn, all-weather tennis court, and facili-ties for fishing on eleven miles of the River Derwent. Nearby attractions include Scarborough Castle (and the busy seaside resort of Scarborough itself), the North Yorkshire Moors Rail-way, Whitby Castle, the historic city of York with its famous Minster, still being lovingly restored after a serious fire in 1984, and, of course, the North Yorkshire Moors National Park all around you.

29

JERVAULX HALL

Address Ripon, North Yorkshire HG4 4PH
Tel: 0677 60235

Nearest town Masham.
Directions The hotel is fourteen miles from Ripon,
so follow the A6108 from Masham to Middleham
and you will find Jervaulx Hall next to Jervaulx
Abbey.
Open from March until mid-November (except for
parties of eight persons or more).
Spring breaks available from time of March opening
until Easter.
Price for dinner, with wine, bed and breakfast for
two – £100–£150.
Credit cards None accepted.
*The hotel is suitable for the disabled; children are welcome,
and dogs by prior arrangement, but they must never be
left alone in the bedrooms.*
Overall mark out of ten 7

Beautifully secluded in the heart of the Yorkshire Dales, yet
only twenty minutes' drive from the main A1, Jervaulx Hall has

achieved an enviable combination of rural charm and homely luxury. It sits on the edge of the Dales National Park, an area of 680 square miles containing some of the most spectacular scenery in northern England.

Despite the hotel's ancient name, taken from the adjoining Jervaulx Abbey which dates back to 1156, the house was built no earlier than the middle of the last century by the Earl of Ailesbury. He wanted a manor house on his 10,000-acre estate and could find no better site than that adjacent to the ruined twelfth-century abbey whose crumbling walls, even in the 1850s, were a veritable riot of brightly coloured marjoram and sunflowers.

The eight-acre garden surrounding the hotel is sheltered from the winds by a tree-covered mound to the north. The main lawn faces south and enjoys the best views across the old abbey and encircling Jervaulx Park. The remainder of the hotel's garden consists of a range of grassed walks and woodland paths which are almost entirely on level ground, offering a good range of strolls and wanders before dinner or after Sunday lunch.

Inside, the hotel has retained much of the informal private house atmosphere which distinguished it in the days before it became a hotel. Both reception rooms have open fires when the weather dictates, and are deliberately furnished in a manner which looks – and feels – more like a private drawing room than a public lounge. The emphasis is on informality throughout the hotel.

The dining room has a soft apricot decor, and a period blue carpet which creates a restful blend of colours. Non-residents are welcome but not encouraged, so one or two days' notice should be given. Dinner is served promptly at eight each evening; there is a single sitting, and you must be down for dinner at least thirty minutes beforehand to place your order. More flexibility of timing would be very welcome, particularly since however long you choose to stay here, dinner, bed and breakfast are included in your tariff. No allowance is made if you want to stay for just bed and breakfast, although the cost of dinner will be deducted from a stay of several nights if you decide to eat elsewhere on one occasion.

Dinner is chosen from a limited set menu, which offers just two or three dishes for each course (plus a vegetable risotto or similar for vegans). The food is simple English fare, opening with something like a Salmon Mousse or Chicken Liver Pâté, and followed by Roast Leg of Lamb or Haddock Barrie with a selection of vegetables. In keeping with the style and informal atmosphere of the hotel as a whole, the wine list is very limited. Neither the gourmet nor the wine connoisseur should consider Jervaulx Hall unless they plan a weekend 'off duty', but for those looking for a more simple kind of English comfort, then this might be the place for you.

Jervaulx Hall has ten bedrooms, all doubles including one ground-floor room opening on to the garden which is suitable for disabled or elderly visitors, or those with dogs. All rooms are spacious and individually furnished and have private bathrooms and shower. All ten have tea- and coffee-making facilities, but the usual luxuries of colour television and direct-dial telephone have been dispensed with in an attempt to ensure residents' holiday breaks really are a completely relaxing 'switch-off'.

The hotel has no leisure facilities of its own, but riding and pony trekking are available at Masham. Golf courses are located at Masham and Bedale, and fishing can be enjoyed locally as well. Nearby attractions include Jervaulx Abbey itself, Middleham Castle, Castle Bolton, Newby Hall, Castle Howard, Bramham Park, Fountains Abbey, Beamish Museum, and the towns of Ripon, Harrogate, Richmond, Helmsley, Durham and, of course, the historic city of York.

30

KILDWICK HALL

Address Kildwick, near Skipton, North Yorkshire
BD20 9AE
Tel: 0535 632244

Nearest town Skipton.
Directions Kildwick Hall is three miles south of
Skipton. From there, travel along the A629
towards Keighley. From Keighley A650 to Kildwick
roundabout in Kildwick and right at the White
Lion. Turn left at top of hill.
Awards AA *** graded; RAC ***; Egon Ronay and
Michelin recommended.
Open throughout the year.
Special breaks for at least two consecutive nights'
stay are available all year round.
Price for dinner, with wine, bed and breakfast for
two – £100–£150.
Credit cards Access, Visa, Amex and Diners.
*The hotel is not suitable for disabled visitors; children and
dogs are welcome.*
Overall mark out of ten 7½

Kildwick Hall lies three miles south of the Yorkshire town of Skipton, often called the Gateway to the Dales. It is a stately old house, with its origins in the early seventeenth century when it was built by the Currer family. The Currers had close connections with the Brontë family, whose literary genius in the nineteenth century has put them among the most renowned former residents of this lovely part of England.

Emily Brontë, probably the most famous member of the family, used the pseudonym 'Currer Bell' on her published works in order to disguise the fact that she was a woman, women authors being frowned upon in highly conservative early Victorian society. A member of the Currer family who owned Kildwick Hall in the last century used to be Emily's teacher and it was from this connection that the first half of her pseudonym originated. The more common 'Bell' surname is believed to have been inspired by the old bell which still hangs over the side entrance to the present hotel to which Emily was a frequent visitor.

The hotel today still has the imposing Jacobean façade which distinguished it in earlier centuries. A weather-beaten coat of arms is sculpted into the red brickwork above the main door, and two huge stone lions stand guard nearby. Inside, the public rooms are large and rather formal. They have lost rather too little of their period 'stiffness' and as a result can feel a bit austere. The dining room, though, is an outstanding example of a traditional English restaurant where formality and discreet personal service are very much part of the enjoyment. Your break at Kildwick Hall can, of course, be as formal or informal as you choose, but for many guests it is precisely for this atmosphere that they come here year after year.

Polished wood panelling dominates the lounge, and richly ornate plasterwork adorns the dining room. The decor is 'busy', with an assortment of oil paintings never failing to catch the eye wherever you glance. French modern cuisine is served from an impressive à la carte menu, and the hotel's growing reputation as one of northern England's best kitchens is not difficult to understand. Kildwick Hall also has a particularly well-stocked cellar.

All evening meals begin with a small complimentary appetizer which changes nightly – a very pleasant little consideration. Hors d'oeuvres proper include a comprehensive range of French specialities, all explained in considerable detail to reflect the painstaking amount of time and effort which has gone into their preparation.

The cuisine is very imaginative and the menu changes monthly. At the time of going to press one of the favourite main dishes is Fresh Breast of French Duckling, Roasted in Fresh Garlic, served on a Bed of Sugared Limes and Lemons and accompanied by a light Madeira Sauce.

Kildwick Hall has seventeen bedrooms, including four large Honeymoon Suites which are extremely popular with newly-weds and romantic couples with memories to celebrate. All the rooms have private bathroom facilities, and two have four-posters. Advance booking is recommended especially if you want to be sure of a Honeymoon Suite.

The hotel has close links with Ilkley Tennis Club, which has indoor and grass courts available, and golf can be enjoyed at a number of local courses through personal introductions by the hotel management. Croquet can be played within the hotel grounds, and horse riding can also be arranged nearby.

Nearby attractions are plentiful, with the most obvious being the magnificent Yorkshire Dales right on your doorstep. Haworth, the area in which the Brontë family lived, is just fifteen minutes' drive away, and also within easy reach by car are Skipton Castle, Ilkley and the surrounding Ilkley Moor, the cities of Leeds and Bradford, and the beautiful Lake District within an hour's drive.

31

KIRKBY FLEETHAM HALL

Address Kirkby Fleetham, Northallerton, North
Yorkshire DL7 0SU
Tel: 0609 748711 Fax: 0609 748747

Nearest town Northallerton.
Directions From the A1, follow signs to Kirkby
Fleetham, about eight miles south of Scotch
Corner. From the village follow a small sign on the
green to 'Kirkby Fleetham Hall' and the hotel is
one mile north of the village, by the church.
Awards AA *** graded; British Tourist Authority
commended; Egon Ronay 76%; Michelin and Ashley
Courtenay recommended.
Special terms for two-night breaks available.
Price for dinner, with wine, bed and breakfast for
two – over £150.
Credit cards Visa, Access, Diners and Amex.
*The hotel is not suitable for the disabled; dogs accepted by
prior arrangment.*
Overall mark out of ten 9

One of the foremost Country House Hotels in northern England,

Kirkby Fleetham Hall has received generous commendation from practically every major British hotel association and guide in the ten years it has been open.

The Manor of Kirkby dates back to before the Norman Conquest of England in 1066. Originally it grew up as a Viking settlement on the banks of the River Swale and in the Domesday Book, in 1086, it was recorded that the manor was then held by one Alfred the Saxon. The estate passed through the hands of several families, including those of Sir Nicholas Stapleton, a knight of the great crusading Order of the Templars who died in 1290. The present house dates back as far as 1600 when the Smelt family built a small manor house that was enlarged considerably towards the end of the seventeenth century.

In 1740 the estate was sold to John Aislabie who, with his son William, improved the gardens considerably, adding both the present lake and terracing, and making cost-effective agricultural units out of the surrounding estate farms. Descendants of the family owned the house up until the end of the last century, and new owners made a number of major structural improvements. Sadly, the interior was allowed to deteriorate in the second half of this century to such a point that the house was completely run down by 1980, although painstaking efforts since then have happily saved the building.

There is a fine dividing line between a Country House Hotel and a larger house which is now a luxury hotel that happens to be in the country. Yet if any hotel in this guide had to be nominated as the one which bridged the two definitions, then this would be it. The public rooms are elegantly furnished without being ostentatious: within the reception hall, formalities are conducted at a huge antique writing desk, while throughout the hotel informal luxury is the order of the day. This atmosphere is maintained efficiently but unobtrusively by Kirkby Fleetham's management team and staff, headed by Stephen Mannock. Their philosophy is simple: 'We like to feel that people come here as guests but that by the time they leave, they're our friends.'

The hotel has twenty-two bedrooms, all en suite and each with the feel of a guest room in a private house rather than a hotel. Abundant flowers – cut from the Hall's own gardens –

are augmented by bought-in sprays which are changed twice weekly, while antique fittings complete the timeless ambience.

From the rooms at the back of the house there is a splendid vista over Kirkby Fleetham's thirty acres of policies. Within the grounds meander several woodland walks, giving the observant guest opportunities to see some of Kirkby Fleetham's surprisingly abundant wildlife. Alternatively, through a period summerhouse, entrance can be gained to an exquisite Victorian kitchen garden, complete with a range of vegetables and fruits as well as herbaceous borders. This provides fresh ingredients for Head Chef David Alton who is making Kirkby Fleetham into one of northern England's foremost restaurants. Principally traditional fare, though prepared in the *nouvelle* style, the hotel's high standards of cuisine are complemented by its polished mahogany tables, bone china, silver cutlery and crystal glasses.

The menu – which is highly original – changes each night. For £29.50 a choice of five starters leads on to a further choice of soups, five main-course options, and a selection of homemade desserts. Particularly mouthwatering are the fish main course options, such as Strips of John Dory and Fresh Salmon on a light Saffron Butter Sauce and a Bed of Buttered Green Vegetables, or Fillet of Sea Trout and Fresh Hake gently poached in White Wine, served on a Cream of Chive Sauce, laced with Smoked Salmon. To round off the savoury dishes, Iced Strawberry Soufflé and a Hot Soufflé of Armagnac accompanied by a Vanilla Anglaise makes an excellent finale. With an all-encompassing 300-wine bin list, guests can choose from 'house' at £8 a bottle, to 'classics' at over £200.

Most outdoor and indoor pursuits are available locally, while clay pigeon shooting and fly fishing (Kirkby Fleetham's lake is well stocked with trout) are offered within the grounds. Nearby attractions include the wide expanses of James Herriot country (the North Yorkshire Moors and dales), Castle Howard, Harewood House and Fountains Abbey.

32

LANGLEY CASTLE

Address Langley-on-Tyne, Hexham,
Northumberland NE47 5LU
Tel: 0434 688888

Nearest town Hexham.
Directions Take the A69 from Carlisle or Newcastle,
heading south along the A686, near Haydon Bridge.
Langley Castle is one and a half miles on the right.
Awards AA selected, RAC ** graded and Egon
Ronay Guide.
Open throughout the year.
Special breaks 'Getaway' two-day half-board breaks
available from 1 November to 31 March. Half-
board weekly rates also on offer.
Price for dinner, with wine, bed and breakfast for
two – £100–£150.
Credit cards Amex, Diners, Visa and Access.
*Children are welcome, as are dogs but the hotel is not
suitable for the disabled.*
Overall mark out of ten 7

In the heart of Northumberland – county of castles – surrounded by ten acres of woodland, stands the imposing yet peaceful Langley Castle, over 600 years old, give or take a decade or two. Believed to be the only medieval fortified castle hotel in England, Langley retains an atmosphere redolent of knights in shining armour, whilst offering the up-to-date luxury that one would expect of a three-star Country House Hotel.

Although a venerable structure – its seven-feet-thick walls built to last and withstand the might of Scots onslaughts – the castle survived a mere fifty years after being built: in 1405 its interior was gutted by fire whereupon it remained untouched until the late nineteenth century. Thus while other castles were being modified according to the prevailing fashions throughout the centuries, Langley Castle continued to retain its genuine medieval character. In a survey of 1542, for instance, it was described as 'a ruined castle with only walls standing, but situated in a very convenient place for the defence against the Scots of Liddesdale and the thieves of Tynedale'.

That Langley exists at all – let alone in all its gloriously restored splendour – is due entirely to the painstaking work and vision of two people – Cadwallader Bates and his wife Josephine. Their monumental task was started in 1895, and Josephine continued it after Cadwallader's death in 1902, finally completing it in 1914. This restoration work became like a mission to Josephine, and the one room which above all others had significance to her was the chapel, which she dedicated to the memory of her late husband. After her own death in 1933, Josephine was finally reunited with her husband, being buried alongside his grave in the castle grounds. Today, the architectural integrity of their work has earned the castle a Grade I listed building status, and a collection of 'before' and 'during' photographs located on the first floor makes a fascinating display.

Imposingly solid by day, and fairy-tale-like at night, illuminated by powerful floodlights, Langley Castle always makes a dramatic impression. Among its more noteworthy features are the magnificent Norman windows in each bedroom; some splendid staircases, including one with a right-hand spiral twist to favour defending swordsmen; and what is purported to be the finest collection of fourteenth-century garderobes (gravity lavatories) in Europe. The drawing room – with its tasteful decor, large tapestries and vast inglenook fireplace – provides a grand yet relaxed setting for enjoying a drink from the adjoining oak-panelled bar. Downstairs, the restaurant is reminiscent of a medieval banqueting hall, but manages to convey an intimate and personal atmosphere. The à la carte dinner menu combines variety with good value – an evening meal working out at around £15 a head, excluding wine. Some intriguing dishes await the unsuspecting: Sir Hubert's Folly, for example, or the delicate flavours of the Blackcurrant Bavarois, speciality of chef Gavin Brown. Disappointingly, the choice of wines is somewhat restricted and a touch on the pricey side. The serving staff, however, are both discreet and friendly.

Langley Castle has eight exclusive bedrooms, some of which have adjoining jacuzzis or saunas. Each has been individually designed to make the most of architectural features such as window seat nooks, gothic doorways and imposing fireplaces. None of the comforts of twentieth-century luxury have been sacrificed, however, and as a personal touch, each bedroom is named after a historical character associated with the castle, such as de Lucy, Radcliffe or Percy. Although each bedroom is different within, the view from all of them over Langley's surrounding woodland policies is equally impressive.

While Langley Castle offers none of the leisure facilities sometimes associated with larger Country House Hotels, there are quiet, unspoilt walks to be had in the surrounding woods, as well as beautiful countryside to be enjoyed in the nearby Border Forest Park and Northumberland National Park. The historic town of Hexham, with its imposing Abbey, is only six miles away, while to the north lies Hadrian's Wall.

33

MALLYAN SPOUT

Address Goathland, Whitby, Yorkshire YO22 5AN
Tel: 0947 86206

Nearest town Whitby.
Directions The hotel is located nine miles from the
coastal town of Whitby and ten miles from the market
town of Pickering. It is signposted two miles off the
main road between the two.
Awards Egon Ronay and AA recommended.
Open throughout the year.
Special breaks Two-day (or longer) special half-
board rates apply all year round.
Price for dinner, with wine, bed and breakfast for
two – under £100.
Credit Cards Visa, Amex, Access and Diners.
*The hotel is unsuitable for disabled visitors; children and
dogs are welcome.*
Overall mark out of ten 6½

Mallyan Spout is an appealing little hotel lying about forty miles
north-east of the historic city of York. Its rather unusual name
comes from a small waterfall which flows into a wooded valley

just a short walk below the hotel. Unlike virtually every other Country House Hotel included in this guide, Mallyan Spout has never been a private residence. It was built during the last years of the nineteenth century as a small hotel and, despite several changes of owner and minor alterations, has operated as a hotel ever since.

The exterior of the building is almost completely covered by dense green ivy; only a small corner of red brickwork can still be seen on the façade, and even the main chimney stack at the right-hand end of the building is obscured. Wherever you go in the hotel, you can see that this house was purpose-built. The public areas, of just the correct proportions, remain simply but comfortably furnished, with velvet armchairs and an interesting selection of old prints rather haphazardly arranged all over the walls. A portrait of Sir Winston Churchill dominates the wall above the smoke-stained stone fireplace in the main living room.

The simple comfort which typifies Mallyan Spout is retained in the dining room, which overlooks the garden and can seat up to sixty people. The room is modern in design and decor, with one or two clashes of style, like the all too obvious radiator beneath an ornate gold-framed mirror (which even features in the hotel's brochure) and the crystal-like chandeliers against an uncomplicated plain ceiling, but the overall effect is pleasing.

Mallyan does its utmost to cater for guests' individual requirements at dinner, and concentrates on providing good home-produced food made from fresh local produce. The chef's speciality is fresh Whitby fish which is bought direct from the quay at Whitby Bay. A set menu and a modest à la carte menu are available each evening, both with an emphasis on fish, and two of the highlights from the set menu are a delicious Mallyan Seafood Terrine to start with (a mousse of local whiting, monk fish, and salmon caviar, all served with a tangy mayonnaise), followed by Whole Grilled Lemon Sole with Parsley Butter. Two popular highlights from the à la carte menu are Breast of Chicken, filled with Herb and Garlic Butter and panfried, and Butterfried Moorland Trout, served with Nut-Brown Butter and Almonds. The choice of wines is reasonable, but the house white at around £7.50 a bottle is excellent value.

Mallyan has twenty-four bedrooms, all with television and private bathroom facilities. The rooms have all been refurbished recently to incorporate Laura Ashley designs. A number of the rooms are rather small, the main exceptions being the deliberately larger doubles which also serve as family rooms. However, most have glorious views across the surrounding Yorkshire countryside which is a reasonable consolation.

The hotel does not have any leisure facilities to speak of, but golf, tennis, sea and freshwater fishing and horse riding can be arranged locally. Mallyan emphasizes the fact that it is an ideal centre for people to come just to relax, get away from town or city life, and enjoy the rural beauty of the surrounding countryside. And indeed it is. The local tourist authority produces a very detailed brochure containing lists of things to see in the immediate area. Nearby attractions include the rugged coastline and resorts of Scarborough and Whitby, and the city of York.

34

MICHAELS NOOK

Address Grasmere, Cumbria LA22 9RP
Tel: 096 65 496

Nearest town Grasmere.
Directions From the south, take exit 36 from the
M6, following the A590 towards Kendal. Turn onto
the A591 and continue through Windermere and
Ambleside towards Keswick. Grasmere village is
signposted to the left; take the first right AFTER the
turn for Grasmere and the hotel will be found on
the right.
A member of the **Pride of Britain** consortium.
Awards Recommended by AA, Egon Ronay,
Michelin, Good Food Guide; Egon Ronay 79%.
Open throughout the year.
Minimum booking at a weekend during the season
is usually three nights, and four nights over a bank
holiday weekend.
Price for dinner, with wine, bed and breakfast for
two – over £200.

Credit cards Amex.
No children under twelve; no dogs in the hotel; no
smoking in the restaurant.
Overall mark out of ten 8

The hotel takes its name from a poem written by local nonpareil, William Wordsworth: 'Upon a forest side at Grasmere Vale there dwelt a shepherd, Michael was his name.' The house is far removed from anything the original Michael might have aspired to, having been built as a summer home by a Lancashire cotton mill magnate in 1859. It has everything that Victorian wealth could buy: beautiful wood panelling and floors, carved door surrounds, mosaics, massive fireplaces and elaborate ceilings. But the atmosphere is nonetheless intimate – the house was after all built for a family – and none of the rooms is over-large or awe inspiring.

Reg Gifford, who opened Michaels Nook as a hotel in 1969, is also an antique dealer and his choice of paintings, furnishings and ornaments complements the house down to the last detail. Everything is geared to comfort – open fires in the bar and in the drawing room with its huge soft sofas, magnificent rugs, flowers and plants.

There are nine double bedrooms, all with their own private bathroom, colour television, radio and direct-dial telephone. Each is individually furnished with the same care and concern for the period found in the rest of the house; some rooms are larger than others while two have four-poster beds. There are also two suites, one twin bedded and the other with a double bed. The bedroom of the first opens on to a private terrace and the sitting room has one of the finest views from the hotel; the other has a study/sitting room and its own patio. Full room service is available. There is a splendid light oak-panelled room, again with an open fire, which can be reserved for private dinner parties or executive meetings.

The Lake District is a popular destination throughout the year. At Michaels Nook there are three acres of quiet and secluded landscaped grounds around the house, with a croquet lawn, Victorian statuary and grassy walkways, with views towards

Scafell Pikes to the west and Furness Fells to the south-west; Helvellyn is just up the road so the hotel is right in the heart of some of the finest walking country and most unspoilt scenery in Britain. There are complementary facilities available from the Wordsworth Hotel down the road which is under the same ownership – you'll find a sauna and solarium as well as a heated indoor swimming pool for a little exercise and relaxation.

One of the major attractions of Michaels Nook is the restaurant which seats just twenty-six people and is widely acclaimed for its imaginative use of fresh produce to create wonderful delicate dishes that delight the palate and the eye. The four-course menu presents such pleasant and exciting combinations as fresh Scottish Scallops with Saffron, or Guinea Fowl and Leek Terrine served en croute with Haw Jelly for starters, followed by a light soup such as Cream of Parsnip and Apple, or Game Consommé with Pheasant Quenelles.

Favourite entrées might include Breast of Wild Mallard with a sauce of Champagne and Pink Peppercorns; a Ragout of Calves' Kidneys with Aran Seed Mustard and home-made Noodles; a Noisette of Lamb with Lamb Sweetbreads on a fresh Garden Herb Sauce; a Pocket of Turbot filled with Prawns, Garlic and young vegetables, roasted and served on a light cream sauce; or perhaps Medallions of Pork Fillet with Green Chartreuse and Black Grapes. A completely new choice is offered each day with a selection of at least three desserts such as Chocolate Marquise with Coffee Bean Sauce, Hot Feuilleté of Apple with Cinnamon Sauce, or Hazelnut Parfait with Raspberry Coulis.

The quality wines are selected by Reg Gifford himself, both for their compatibility with his menus and for their value. His cellar is home to some wines of real distinction and can rise to every occasion.

The polished mahogany tables are laid with fine bone china and heavy silverware, candelabra and fresh flowers. The open fire, deep red walls, chandeliers and thick carpet give the dining room a sumptuous but far from inhibiting atmosphere in which to enjoy eating a meal that would be recommended by the most fastidious of gourmets.

Surrounded by such cosseting and luxury, to say nothing of

the uplifting beauty of the Lake District, it is unlikely that guests will want to do too much rushing about on the tourist trail, but local attractions include Rydal Mount and Dove Cottage where Wordsworth lived and worked for many years, and the Wordsworth Museum is just along the road. The little seventeenth-century house where Beatrix Potter wrote the Peter Rabbit books is near Sawrey at Hawkshead, or perhaps a gentle trip on Coniston Water in the National Trust's handsomely renovated steam yacht *Gondola* would be more in keeping with the tone set by Michaels Nook.

MIDDLETHORPE HALL

Address Bishopthorpe Road, York YO2 1QB
Tel: 0904 641241 Fax: 0904 620176

Nearest town York.
Directions Middlethorpe Hall is situated one and a
half miles outside York, alongside York
racecourse. From the south by car, Middlethorpe is
reached by following the signs 'North' on the M1,
and M18, A1 (M), A1 and A64, leaving at the exit
marked 'York/West A1036, racecourse and
Bishopthorpe'.
A member of the **Prestige Hotels** consortium.
Awards AA *** (red) graded; RAC Blue Ribbon;
British Tourist Authority commendation; Queen's
Award to Industry for Export Achievement 1987.
Open throughout the year.
Special breaks Two-day half-board Champagne
Breaks available from November until March.

Price for dinner, with wine, bed and breakfast for two – over £150.
Credit cards Access, Visa, Amex and Diners.
The hotel is not suitable for the disabled; children under eight years and dogs not permitted.
Overall mark out of ten 9½

With its magnificent location just one and a half miles from the historic city of York, overlooking York racecourse, Middlethorpe Hall was the second decaying old manor house to be rescued by Historic House Hotels and transformed into a truly first-class luxury Country House Hotel within the space of a decade. The other one, Bodysgallen Hall, is located in north Wales and also featured in this guide.

Middlethorpe was positively wrested from the hands of vandals when bought in 1980. The previous owners had turned it into a 1960s nightclub. Paint was layered over the oak panels, disco lights erected on the cornices, and the seventeenth-century walls resounded to the blare of pop. Numerous acts of architectural vandalism had to be undone in lengthy and expensive operations before the glories of this magnificent home could again be enjoyed in 1984. Thankfully they were, and the end result is one of Britain's finest Country House Hotels.

Although a few outbuildings date back to the 1680s, and traces of timbers going back as far as a couple of centuries before that have been found, the main structure of Middlethorpe Hall was built in 1699 by local industrialist Thomas Barlow. He was not spared long to enjoy his attractive new property as he died whilst on a Grand Tour of Europe with his son in 1713.

From the moment visitors to Middlethorpe Hall are greeted at the door by the uniformed doormen on their arrival at the hotel, they invariably get the impression that time has stood still – an impression which lingers throughout their stay. The hotel is exceptionally well maintained, and the public rooms resemble those tantalizing rooms in a stately home where you'd love to sit down but are never allowed to because of infuriating rope cordons.

The large main drawing room is a positive treat, with its

elegant crystal chandelier and oil portraits all around. This is where pre-dinner drinks are served by the footmen. Whatever room you are in, little touches like potted plants and open magazines make it feel so much more like a home than a hotel. The staff are discreet but attentive; nothing is ever too much trouble at Middlethorpe.

The hotel has two restaurants, the main dining room on the ground floor, the more formal of the two with magnificent views overlooking the gardens, and the grill room downstairs. Reservations are compulsory, dress must be formal, and ten days to a fortnight are recommended for advance bookings to be sure of a table. The grill room serves a three-course table d'hôte menu, representing a more traditional approach to the bill of fare, and a pianist provides a gentle background music most evenings.

For some of the finest gourmet cooking in northern England a visit to the main dining room really is a must. The extensive menus are changed frequently and the emphasis is on such touches as crisp vegetables, exotic sauces and excellent presentation by chef Kevin Francksen. Particularly recommended are the Collops of Venison and Scallops, or the Trio of Veal, Beef and Venison Fillets. An extensive wine list is available, although the only real minus point so far as the main dining room is concerned is the fact that some of the more common wines are a little overpriced.

Middlethorpe Hall has thirty bedrooms, eleven in the main house, the rest in the adjacent eighteenth-century stable courtyard or beautifully restored Gardener's Cottage. All are individually designed, and the standard of furnishings, attention to detail and overall quality are outstanding. Each room has colour television, direct-dial telephone and its own bathroom facilities, complete with brass fittings, wooden toilet seats and high-quality toiletries.

The house is set in twenty-six acres of secluded woodland and garden, offering endless possibilities for evening strolls or, for the less energetic, a croquet lawn is available. Golf, horse riding and fishing can also be arranged nearby. Nearby attractions are numerous, although the most obvious is historic York with its famous Minster, narrow little streets and crowded antique shops. Other places of interest are Castle Howard, architecturally one of the most splendid houses in England, Beningborough Hall (a National Trust property), Selby Abbey, Fountains Abbey (one of the most important medieval abbeys in Europe) and Newby Hall, with its remarkable interiors crafted by Robert Adam in the late eighteenth century.

36

ROOKHURST

Address Gayle, Hawes, North Yorksire DL8 3RT
Tel: 0969 667 454

Nearest town Hawes.
Directions Leave either the M6 (junction 37) or the
A1 when you see signposts for the A684. Rookhurst
is located half a mile south of the little town of
Hawes, midway between the two main roads.
Awards AA two star; British Tourist Authority three
Crowns; Ashley Courtenay recommended.
Open throughout the year, excluding Christmas.
Special **winter breaks** available.
Price for dinner, with wine, bed and breakfast for
two – under £100.
Credit cards None accepted.
*The hotel is unsuitable for the disabled; there are no
facilities for under twelve year olds, and dogs (except guide
dogs) are not allowed. No smoking in the bedrooms or
restaurant.*
Overall mark out of ten 9

Rookhurst looks like a solid old manor house but, in fact, it was originally built as a farmhouse in 1670. An exterior stone inscription bears the date 1734, but recent research has revealed that this was when most of the internal walls, wood panelling and the rear of the house were added. For a couple of centuries the old farmhouse was known as the West End House, and was owned by the Whaley family whose local connections date back to the early fifteenth century.

The house was derelict for a couple of generations prior to 1869 when barrister Henry Whaley retired from the City of London and found that he 'required a residence in Gayle befitting his position'. He commissioned a firm of local builders (whose descendants still live in the village) to add the present eastern wing to the house, in a grand Victorian neo-Gothic style which turned out to be quite unique to the Yorkshire Dales. Henry Whaley also adopted the name Rookhurst (after the resident rookery) and his family remained in the house until 1973.

When the house was purchased and made into a guest house, work was needed to change it from a family home into letting accommodation. It was sold in 1984 and again more work carried out before it became a hotel. All the public rooms are furnished with antiques; the decor is discreet and the atmosphere very relaxed. The view across the garden from the large bay windows in the main lounge has changed little over the last couple of centuries, and the charm of the place remains as great as ever. The Victorian dining room faces east and on sunny mornings the shafts of sunlight pouring through the large bay windows give a wonderful warm tranquil feeling.

Breakfast is grilled to order with lots of freshly made coffee or tea. The owner Iris Van Der Steen and her husband Joe themselves now live in the beautiful old house. Iris is English but Joe's ancestors were Flemish weavers who came to England in 1600 and settled in the East End of London until the turn of this century.

Dinner is served at 7.30 in the evening and the menu is changed every day. The restaurant is not open to non-residents. A typical meal starts with Wensleydale Cheese and Prawns in sauce, or onion soup with toasted cheese. The main course can be chosen from three or four options and includes specialities like Red Salmon Steak cooked in Cream, and local Lamb Chops with Redcurrant and Port Wine Sauce. There is a fish main course every night and vegetarian food is provided on request.

All the double bedrooms have private facilities: colour TV, mini bar, tea and coffee making facilities. The six bedrooms are individually furnished – one has a brass four-poster, another a large mahogany four-poster, others have half-tester beds. The Georgian bedrooms are large but have low-beamed ceilings. The Victorian bedrooms, on the other hand, have very high ceilings and stone mullion bay windows. The bridal suite has the additional luxury of an authentic Doulton bathroom suite with its original fittings and mahogany surround, which dates back to 1903.

Iris Van Der Steen has not altered the fundamental charm of Rookhurst by adding a plethora of leisure facilities; rather, peace and quiet are the main attractions of this hotel. Nearby places to visit include Bolton Castle (where Mary Queen of Scots was imprisoned for a time); Middleham, once home to the famous English usurper Richard III; Jervaulx Abbey; Skipton Castle (nine hundred years old and still fully roofed), Bowes Museum, near Barnard Castle; White Scar caves; and of course the beautiful Yorkshire dales and Herriot country.

37

ROWLEY MANOR

Address Little Weighton, near Hull, North
Humberside HU20 3XR
Tel: 0482 848248 Fax: 0482 849900

Nearest town Hull
Directions From the M62, follow the A63 until the
junction signposted for Beverley. Head for the village
of South Cave, and turn right at staggered junction
opposite clock tower. Follow the road up through
trees, go across Riplingham crossroads and take
next left. The hotel is signposted just at the top of
a steep bend.
Awards AA and RAC *** graded; recommended by
Egon Ronay and Ashley Courtenay.
Open throughout the year.
Weekend breaks are available all year round.
Price for dinner, with wine, bed and breakfast for
two – under £100.
Credit cards Access, Visa, Amex and Diners.

The hotel is not suitable for disabled visitors; children and dogs are welcome
Overall mark out of ten 8

Set in thirty-four acres of lawns, parkland and beautifully kept rose gardens, Rowley Manor is an extremely attractive Georgian building in the heart of the Yorkshire Wolds. It provides a perfect haven from many of the stresses of the modern world, combined with the comforts of a well-appointed Country House Hotel in an extremely attractive part of northern England.

Rowley Manor was built in the early seventeenth century as a rectory for the small church which can still be seen in the grounds today. The busy life of the parish came to an abrupt end later that century when the rector persuaded all his parishioners to join him on the long voyage to Massachusetts, then one of the flourishing new emigration centres of the American colonies. Once there, he and the survivors established the settlement which became known as Rowley Massachusetts. In later years Rowley Manor was to become the home of Philmer Wilson, a senior member of the family which established the Ellerman Wilson Shipping Line.

All the public rooms are furnished in period style, and frequently adorned with antiques. The main lounge is wood panelled and has an elaborate carved fireplace which forms a magnificent frame to the roaring log fire during the colder winter months. Gold-framed oil portraits adorn the walls, and subtle lighting creates a marvellously informal atmosphere in which to sit back and relax with an after-dinner coffee or liqueur.

The dining room is the largest public room and has a very traditional decor, with period-style furniture and solid, polished wooden doors which contrast well with the dark wallpaper. Wood panelling frames the fireplaces and, as with the main lounge, a number of original oil paintings finish off the room splendidly. Up to eighty can be served at once and Rowley Manor's dining room is extremely popular with non-residents in a ratio to residents of approximately three to one. The management recommends at least a week's advance booking.

Rowley Manor specializes in serving fine fresh English cuisine, and Head Chef Martin Collis's fine à la carte menu is presented on thick parchment-type paper. There are about fifteen starters to choose from, ranging from the standard selection of fruit juices and seafood cocktails to more elaborate dishes like Courgettes filled with Savoury Mince, and an exquisite plate of Smoked Salmon Cornets filled with Prawns and Crabmeat, served in a subtle Mousseline Sauce.

Half a dozen fish choices follow, and you may prefer a dish of King Prawns served in Garlic Butter, or even a large grilled Halibut Steak covered with a Tomato, Asparagus and White Wine Sauce as a main dish rather than a fish course. Before making up your mind, do at least have a read through the detailed list of main dishes proper. There are generally about twenty main dishes available, including at least half a dozen steaks ranging from a massive 1lb T-bone to a more manageable sirloin cooked in garlic. Other options include traditional English specialities like duckling, venison, honey roast lamb and loin of pork, and there is also a small range of vegetarian dishes available at a very reasonable set price which compare favourably with the meat dishes.

Rowley Manor has sixteen bedrooms: all but three rooms are double or twin-bedded, and all have private bathroom facilities, colour television, complimentary toiletries and direct-dial telephone. As an added bonus, all the rooms have good views across the surrounding thirty-four acres of private estate attached to the hotel, and a number have antique four-posters to add that little extra to a special break.

The hotel's only leisure facility is a solarium, although most common sports such as golf and fishing can be arranged locally, and other nearby attractions are numerous. These include the town of Beverley, with its superb old Minster, the Museum of Army Transport, Skidby Windmill, Hull Marine and Maritime Heritage Centre, Spurn Point, the magnificent Humber Bridge just ten minutes' drive away, and the cities of Hull and York within an easy drive.

38

SHARROW BAY

Address Penrith, Cumbria CA10 2LZ
Tel: 07684 86301 Fax: 07684 86439

Nearest town Penrith.

Directions Leave the M6 at junction 40 and follow
signs towards Martindale. After Pooley Bridge it is
only a few miles along the edge of Ullswater to
Sharrow Bay.

A member of the **Relais et Châteaux** consortium.

Awards AA *** (red) graded and two rosettes for
food; British Tourist Authority commended; major
awards include Egon Ronay's Hotel of the Year 1974
and Restaurant of the Year 1980 (the only British
hotel ever to have won both Gold awards); Egon
Ronay/*Sunday Times* Taste of England Award 1983;
British Academy of Gastronomes Chef Laureate
Award 1986; Ackerman Clover Leaf Award 1987;
Catey Special Award 1988.

Open from early March until late November

Price for dinner, with wine, bed and breakfast for
two – over £150.
Credit cards None accepted.
The hotel is unsuitable for the disabled; children under
fourteen and dogs are not allowed.
Overall mark out of ten 9

Judging by the number of major awards the Sharrow Bay hotel
has won over the last decade or so, it is not difficult to understand why this is one of the best all-round Country House
Hotels in England. The main hotel building is basically an early
Victorian mansion, built in 1840, but a cottage was known to
have stood here in the eighteenth century and the house was
built on the same site to include part of the original cottage.

Sharrow Bay remained a private residence until 1949 when it
was turned into a Country House Hotel. Resident proprietors
Francis Coulson and Brian Sack are, this year, entering their
forty-third season at Sharrow Bay and have come a long way
since the bleak post-war years when they took over the house.
This hotel was the first of its kind in the UK and, they claim,
the definitive Country House Hotel which started the whole
movement in this country.

The style of life at Sharrow Bay is unhurried and traditional.
There are two beautiful public lounges where afternoon tea,
complete with home-made scones, jam, fresh cream, cakes and
unlimited tea, is served. Decor and furnishings are a relaxing
blend of browns and golds, although to many people's tastes
the public rooms and bedrooms alike are a little cluttered, with
ornaments and bits and pieces accumulated over four decades
in the hotel business. The enormous picture window in the
drawing room is a delight, offering an ever-changing panorama
across the lake to the Martindale Fells.

Asked to name her favourite restaurant in 1984, romantic
novelist Barbara Cartland had no hesitation in calling Sharrow
Bay 'one of the most romantic and exciting places in the British
Isles. The food defies description . . .' English-style food is
served, and at least three weeks' advance booking is rec-

ommended for non-residents. Lavish praise is more than deserved for the exquisite five- or six-course table d'hôte menu.

Nearly a dozen starters include a selection of Sharrow speciality soups and a range of more substantial hors d'oeuvres, which includes a delicious Duck Foie Gras served on a bed of dressed salad, and a Terrine of Fresh Salmon and Sole, served with Salmon Caviar and Tomato Vinaigrette. It is worth noting that there is no additional surcharge for the traditionally more expensive options such as smoked salmon or foie gras.

A modest set fish course, followed by a fruit sorbet, precedes the outstanding list of main dishes. Main courses include Fresh Local Salmon, Roast Lancashire Duck, Cumberland Pork Cutlets and Fresh Scallops from the Kyle of Lochalsh, all cooked in a unique style and dressed with sauces richer than you ever thought possible. If you have room for a sweet, the laden sweet trolley is one of the best-known features of the hotel; indeed, Egon Ronay once asked Francis Coulson to present an Old English Regency Syllabub at Maxims in Paris.

Menu specialities do, of course, change from season to season, but whatever you opt for the overall presentation and quality is unrivalled in northern England. Once you've eaten dinner at Sharrow Bay it is not difficult to understand why the Consumers' Association Good Food Guide repeatedly awards the restaurant one of its highest ratings anywhere in England.

Sharrow Bay has a total of twenty-eight bedrooms, including six singles, available in the main hotel building and in several renovated outbuildings in the immediate vicinity. The Edwardian Lodge gatehouse is about 400 yards from the hotel and has three suites and one twin-bedded room. About 100 yards from the hotel lies the aptly named Cottage in the Grounds, a delightful little cottage with one suite, one twin and one small single. For visitors looking for a little extra privacy or seclusion, the hotel also has a seventeenth-century cottage, fully furnished and available for only one couple at a time, and also the Bank House, a converted seventeenth-century farmhouse, about a mile from the main hotel. Breakfast and afternoon tea are served here, but lunch and dinner must be taken at the Sharrow Bay.

All bedrooms are furnished to the highest standards, although one or two rooms in the main hotel do not yet have private bathrooms. Television comes as standard, and little racks of antique porcelain and pieces of period furniture give each room a distinctly individual touch. Virtually all the rooms, particularly those in the main building and Bank House, have breathtaking views across Ullswater. Sharrow Bay was given a special award by the AA in 1977 for having the best views of any hotel in the United Kingdom. Whichever part of this marvellous hotel you choose to stay in, advance booking by at least two months is essential. Amongst Sharrow Bay's many endearing points are its traditional English breakfast and afternoon tea. In a stylish way the hotel is keeping alive two of England's time-honoured, often underrated customs.

Nearby attractions include the market town of Penrith seven miles away, the city of Carlisle about twenty-five miles away, Hadrian's Wall to the east of Carlisle, Wordsworth's cottage eighteen miles away, Beatrix Potter's house where the natural beauty of Cumbria inspired her to write her numerous classic children's tales about Peter Rabbit and his friends, and the Long Meg stone circle near Penrith.

39

UPLANDS

Address Haggs Lane, Cartmel, English Lakes
LA11 6HD
Tel: 05395 36248

Nearest town Grange-over-Sands.
Directions Leave the M6 at junction 36 and follow
the signs to Grange-over-Sands. In Grange go past
the train station (on your left), up the hill, and turn
right at the Crown Apartments. Go straight across
crossroads near here into Grange Fell road, past the
golf course, and turn right at T-junction for
Cartmel. Uplands is a little way up this road on the
right.
Awards AA rosette for food.
Open mid-February until about 2 January.
Special breaks Mid-week breaks are available
outside the main summer season.
Price for dinner, with wine, bed and breakfast for
two – £100–£150.
Credit cards Access, Visa and Amex.
The hotel is unsuitable for disabled visitors; children under

*eight are not allowed; dogs are allowed, but only in the
bedrooms.*

Overall mark out of ten 7

Standing in two acres of garden, with magnificent views far
across Morecambe Bay estuary, Uplands almost qualifies as the
smallest hotel featured in this guide. With only five double
bedrooms, accommodating a maximum of ten residents at a
time, the hotel is never crowded or noisy, and consequently
resident proprietors Diana and Tom Peter haven't had to work
too hard to retain an intimately informal atmosphere.

The house was built around the beginning of this century for
a British admiral, and as such is a solid, functional building with
few architectural points of interest. The present owners altered
the building considerably when they bought it in 1984: the staircase was moved, several walls were knocked down to make the
dining room and lounge much bigger, a completely new hall,
kitchen and cold room were added, and the house was completely replumbed and rewired.

Shades of pink, grey and blue have been used throughout
the ground-floor rooms, and these pale pastel colours contrast
charmingly with the numerous Impressionist prints which came
from the Metropolitan Museum of Art in New York. The whole
effect defies expectations you may have of a Country House
Hotel, both in terms of the distinctly modern interior design and
the genuinely informal atmosphere which prevails throughout
your stay because there are so few residents. But it is a very
pleasant place overall and one to which many people return.

The restaurant seats up to thirty, most of whom are non-
residents, and in keeping with the rest of the ground floor the
decor comprises pale grey walls and pink curtains; more pink-
framed Impressionist prints enhance the walls. The style of
cooking is best described as modern British, and the four-course
table d'hôte menu changes nightly. Prospective guests should
note that simple bed and breakfast is not available; all tariffs
include dinner, bed and full English breakfast.

New speciality starters are constantly being thought up but
two typical dishes are Fresh Squid, with the tentacles filled with

a rich Stuffing made up of Tomatoes, Garlic, Onion and Fresh Basil, all served with a Chive and Cranberry Sauce. You may prefer instead, though, a more traditional Gravlax – Fillet of Salmon marinated in Hazelnut Oil, Brandy Sugar, Salt and Dill – all served with mustard and a thick home-made dill mayonnaise.

A soup or fish course follows, which may be anything from Lemon and Mint Soup to Poached Monkfish served with Cucumber and Dill Sauce. There are generally three options on the list of main dishes. Marinated Local Wood Pigeon, dressed with Pear Purée and Lemon Thyme Sauce is an unusual option but you may prefer something more traditional like Roast Norfolk Duck or Roast Sirloin of Lakeland Beef. One of the most original creations from the Uplands kitchen is one which comprises generous Medallions of Fillet Beef and Pork, stuffed with Gruyère and Parma Ham and served with Mushrooms and Marsala Sauce.

Uplands has five double bedrooms at present, but there are no plans to destroy the intimate atmosphere by adding any more. The existing rooms, however, have impressive views over the surrounding two-acre garden or Morecambe Bay estuary. Each one is individually furnished in a relatively modern style and complete with comfortable accessories like colour television, hairdryer, a generous supply of reading matter and a Travel Scrabble set. Three have private shower and toilet facilities, and one has a full bathroom.

The main attraction of a small Country House Hotel like Uplands in this part of England is the natural beauty of the Lake District all around you. The two nearest villages are appealing for the casual visitor who hasn't come on holiday to indulge in any 'heavy-duty' sightseeing: Cartmel (about a mile away) has an attractive eleventh-century priory, and Grange-over-Sands (about two miles away) is a relatively unspoilt Victorian seaside resort. The town of Kendal is a short drive away, and there are one or two fine old stately homes in the area including Holker Hall, Levens Castle and Sizergh Castle.

Wales

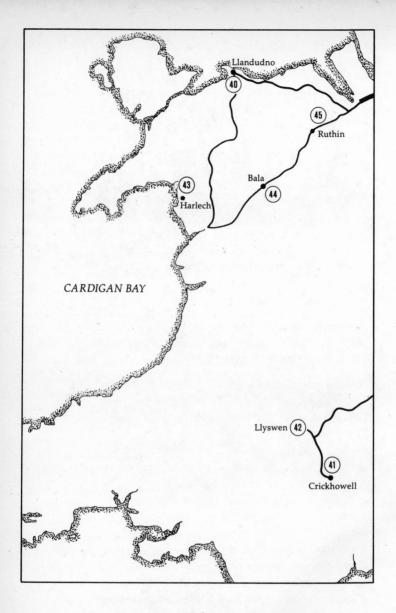

Wales

40

BODYSGALLEN HALL

Address Llandudno, Gwynedd, North Wales LL30
1RS
Tel: 0492 584466 Fax: 0492 582519

Nearest town Llandudno.
Directions Follow the A55 into north Wales from
Chester through Colwyn Bay and down towards
Conwy as far as the junction with the A470. Take
the A470 north, past Llandudno Junction, and the
turn-off for Bodysgallen Hall will be clearly marked
on your right after a few miles.
A member of the **Prestige Hotels** consortium.
Awards *Good Hotel Guide* César Award; RAC Blue
Ribbon; AA *** (red) graded; British Tourist
Authority commendation
Open throughout the year.
Special breaks Summer breaks from May to
1 November for three days half-board or longer;
Winter Champagne breaks from mid-October until
March – two days half-board for two.

Price for dinner, with wine, bed and breakfast for two – over £150.
Credit cards All major cards accepted.
Children under the age of eight only accepted at the discretion of the management; dogs are not allowed except in the Courtyard suites.
Overall mark out of ten 9

Bodysgallen Hall embodies the spirit of a true British Country House Hotel. It stands on a hill looking down on the grand site of Conwy Castle, and on a clear day you can see as far as the mountains of Snowdonia. The earliest part of the present hotel was built in the thirteenth century, and was once used as a lookout by soldiers serving the English kings of Conwy Castle. Today it is reached by a narrow, winding old stone staircase and is used for little more than admiring the truly outstanding views in all directions.

The idea for the house came soon after Conwy Castle itself was built, when there was a need for a smaller castle to act as a watchtower and guard the southern approach slopes to the main castle. Bodysgallen Hall's history is thereafter lost until the Elizabethan era when the Mostyn family, who owned the house, gained control of more of the immediate area. Richard Mostyn rose to become High Sheriff of Caernarvonshire, but with the marriage of his daughter Margaret to Hugh Wynn the house came into the possession of the much stronger Wynn family.

The main body of the hotel was built in the seventeenth century under the auspices of the Wynns and there are a total of five storeys, including the attic and cellars, dating from this time. Pink sandstone, quarried from a nearby field, has been used throughout the hotel's long history for any building or restoration work. The skilful restoration work which has been undertaken this century on both the house and surrounding gardens has earned a number of major awards for the owners and the architects. All work has been carried out in a way that emphasizes the natural beauty of the house, and both furnishings and paintings have been chosen carefully for all the public rooms and bedrooms alike in order to ensure that a warm and comfortable atmosphere is retained.

The hotel was only opened in 1982, and in the space of a single season firmly established itself as one of Britain's top Country House Hotels – with a pleasing emphasis on special romantic breaks. Advance booking of at least six months is normally essential, particularly if you have a preference for any given room or suite. Even for dinner, if you are a non-resident, a fortnight's notice is generally required.

Bodysgallen House has nineteen supremely comfortable bedrooms, each with its own private bathroom facilities and furnished in elegant Edwardian style. Colour television, direct-dial telephone and trouser press are included as standard. Courtyard suites, just off the main body of the hotel, are available for up to four persons. The larger suites have two or more bedrooms and are furnished to the same high standards as the rest of the hotel.

Two of the finest public rooms in the hotel are the grand entrance hall and the main drawing-room on the first floor. Both have authentic period oak wall panelling, stone mullioned windows, and the drawing-room has a very striking ornate seventeenth-century fireplace, complete with Latin inscription, Delft tiles and the original family's coat of arms up above it. Small touches like the mahogany-cased grandfather clock in the reception area and the original oil paintings all around make a big difference to the general atmosphere of the hotel.

The hotel has two dining-rooms, but most meals are served in the larger of the two which can accommodate seventy people at any one time. The cooking is British Country House style, and the dining-room decor is in keeping with the period feel of the rest of the house. Local produce is used wherever possible, but in striving for the very highest standards of international cuisine chef Martin James does look as far afield as Scotland for some of his steaks and the continent for some of the more exotic herbs.

Welsh lamb, though, has been a traditional speciality of Bodysgallen Hall for centuries and is one of the many treats waiting for you on the impressive table d'hôte menu. Vegetables are usually cooked lightly so that they retain their crispness, though anything can be cooked as you like it to suit your preferences. A couple of recommended specialities from the menu are Strips of Chicken lightly roasted in Scotch Whisky, and Poached Fillet of Conwy Sea Trout with Tomato, Sea Salt and Parsley. In addition, the hotel has a really outstanding wine list, easily one of the finest of any Country House included in this guide with nearly 300 vintages to choose from.

Nearby attractions include Conwy and Harlech Castles, the towns of Colwyn Bay and Chester, the huge public gardens of Bodnant, Caernarfon Castle and the Snowdonia National Park.

41

GLIFFAES

Address Crickhowell, Powys, Wales NP8 1RH
Tel: 0874 730371 Fax: 0874 730463

Nearest town Crickhowell.
Directions From Abergavenny, follow the A40 towards Brecon. Two and a half miles west of Crickhowell, you will see the hotel signposted on your right, turn left and drive a mile to Gliffaes gates.
Awards AA *** graded.
Open from the middle Friday in March until the end of December.
Special breaks Good discounts for full-board stays of a week or longer.
Price for dinner, with wine, bed and breakfast for two – under £100.
Credit cards Access, Visa, Amex and Diners.

The hotel is unsuitable for disabled visitors; children are welcome but dogs are not allowed in the hotel – outdoor kennels are available.

Overall mark out of ten 7

Relaxed informality is assured at the Gliffaes Country House Hotel. Lying between the River Usk and the Myarth Hill, it is this position which gives the hotel its rather unusual name: Gliffaes is a rather contorted variation of Gwlydd Faes, meaning literally 'the dewy field' in Welsh. As you will surely see on any chilly morning, the river mists rise with the morning light and become trapped by the hillside so that they fall as heavy dew on the surrounding fields. A twelfth-century chronicler, Giraldus Cambrenis, first recorded a variation on the Gliffaes name, but it was another eight centuries before the present house was built.

The house was the brainchild of a Reverend West, and constructed as a secluded family home between 1883 and 1885. The Reverend had travelled extensively throughout Europe and beyond, and had developed a particular appreciation for the Italian style of architecture, so much so that traces of Italian influence can be perceived in the hotel's intricate stonework today. The campanile at each end of the exterior is a distinctly Venetian touch.

The house has passed through several hands in the twentieth century, and in 1936 new owners Mr and Mrs Ernest Beard first opened their home to paying guests. The standards and facilities have been built up slowly since then and, indeed, maintained and extended by the present owners Nick and Peta Brabner since they acquired outright ownership of the hotel in 1972.

One of the most obvious features of Gliffaes today, as it has been for over a century and a half, is its magnificent gardens. These were planned and laid out by the Reverend West's father in the 1840s, and it was his love and appreciation of rare trees which undoubtedly made the gardens the special place you can enjoy today. W. H. West was a prominent member of the Breconshire Agricultural Society and rose to be High Sheriff of the county for a year in 1833.

Later Victorian residents added a labyrinth of gravel paths, small lawns and tasteful little shrub gardens. The driveway alone stretched over a quarter of a mile, flanked by rhododendrons, and it must have been quite a spectacular sight to drive up in an open carriage at the height of summer when everything was in bloom. An interesting thought is that at one stage fourteen gardeners were in full-time employment just to keep the grounds looking in pristine condition. The gardens today still look splendid, although the current owners reckon just twenty hours' work every week throughout the year is enough to keep the twenty-nine acres well maintained.

Most of Gliffaes has succumbed to the modern luxury of central heating, and the public rooms also have the more traditional log fire when the temperature outside requires it. There are nineteen bedrooms in all, all with private bathroom facilities and each offering a charming view of the rolling Welsh countryside all around. Within the hotel grounds, a lodge has recently been converted to provide an additional three double bedrooms.

The main public room is a huge ground-floor sitting room, furnished in a curious symmetrical fashion and opening into the drawing room; little touches like an old copper pan hanging by the fireplace contribute to the period feel. From the comfortable drawing room, French windows open into an attractive sun lounge with a delightful terrace for guests to sit back and enjoy the garden during the summer months.

Few pieces of period furniture survive in any of the public rooms, with the emphasis more on modern-day comfort. Nevertheless, the decor is pleasing and it is a supremely comfortable and relaxing hotel. The oak-panelled dining room can seat up to sixty-five guests, and it too has a large terrace offering stunning views far across the Brecon countryside and down to the River Usk about 150 feet below. Food is served in traditional Country House style, although continental influences can be detected. The chef clearly prefers to concentrate his energies on quality rather than quantity, with the result that only a limited à la carte choice is available each evening in preference to a full table d'hôte menu.

The range of starters is imaginative, but an obvious speciality is the Gravlax dish composed of Fresh Usk salmon marinated with Dill and served with a Dill and Mustard Sauce. Local salmon features again as a main dish, and an interesting choice would be the Breast of Duckling cooked with a Blackcurrant and Lemon Sauce.

Nearby attractions are plentiful: for the sportsperson, fishing facilities are superb (the Usk is famous for its wild brown trout), there is a hard tennis court with resident professional on hand, and riding, golf, bowls, boating, climbing, caving, bird-watching, gliding and even hang-gliding can all be easily arranged through the hotel reception. Within an easy drive you can visit Newport, Abergavenny and the Welsh capital, Cardiff, with all it has to offer.

42

LLANGOED HALL

Address Llyswen, Brecon, Powys LD3 0YP
Tel: 0874 754525 Fax: 0874 754545

Nearest town Llyswen.
Directions Llangoed Hall is situated eleven miles
south of Builth Wells and eleven miles north-east of
Brecon on the A470, the main road between Cardiff
and Builth Wells.
Open throughout the year
Special breaks Winter Champagne breaks offered.
Price for dinner, with wine, bed and breakfast for
two – over £150.
Credit cards All major credit cards accepted.
*No children under eight allowed. Dogs can be kennelled
in the stable block by prior arrangement. The hotel is not
suitable for the disabled.*
Overall mark out of ten 9

For over 1400 years, the buildings at Llangoed Hall have vari-
ously fulfilled just about every purpose other than use as a
hotel. Some historians believe that the Hall was built on the site
of Wales's legendary White Palace, or Parliament. Following

a period of several hundred years' ecclesiastical ownership, a mansion was constructed on the estate by Sir Henry Williams in 1632. His motto 'Gloriam Dei Cano' and coat of arms can be seen over the hotel's south portico. A sudden twist of fate changed the estate's ownership in 1800 when a certain John MacNamara won Llangoed Hall in a gambling bout. The present mansion, which dates from 1913, was designed by Sir Clough Williams-Ellis, who later created Portmeirion, the curious Italianate village in north Wales. Sir Bernard Ashley wrote about Country Houses '. . . vital is the setting. A drive long enough to leave all cares upon the highway behind you. A park with tall trees, sentinels to the peace that awaits you . . .' This is precisely the effect of the gracious drive at Llangoed Hall, and although the size of the estate has decreased since the staggering 5400 acres it comprised last century, Wye Valley remains a glorious backdrop for Llangoed Hall's well-proportioned buildings and their near surroundings. Clough Williams-Ellis would not be disappointed today: the comforts and pleasures that would have greeted visitors here in the 1920s are still in evidence, but with a considerable degree of modern luxury thrown in.

A central feature of Llangoed Hall's internal construction is a 95-foot-long pillared gallery, which houses a collection of nineteenth- and twentieth-century paintings belonging to the hotel's current owner Sir Bernard Ashley, Chairman of Laura Ashley plc. These paintings include works by Augustus John, Dame Laura Knight and members of the early twentieth-century Scottish School of Art. Given the owner's business connections, it's not surprising that the hotel's twenty-three spacious bedrooms are all superbly decorated in Laura Ashley fabrics and furnishings. The views from Llangoed Hall's bedrooms over the tree-lined valley slopes are wonderful, especially when autumn colours are in full display.

Public rooms at the Hall include the great hall and the morning room – all havens of comfort and peace – as well as a Jacobean panelled library, ideal for curling up with a book by the fire or playing a game of cards or snooker.

Llangoed's dining room offers modern classical cuisine, together with some of the best fare that Wales can supply. The six-course dinner menu is changed regularly, and all dishes are based around the use of fresh local produce. In season, the hotel's own walled garden supplies fresh vegetables and herbs. An illustration of Master Chef Mark Salter's talents could comprise Timbale of Chicken Mousse wrapped in Courgette served with Wild Scottish Chanterelle and a Split Hazelnut Sauce, followed by Fillets of Red Mullet filled with a Pea Purée and Fish Mousse served with fresh Lobster and a Vegetable and Samphire Dressing, then Red Wine Granita. A main course could consist of Fillet of Beef topped with Lentil Purée served with sautéed Potatoes, Glazed Shallots and Thyme Broth. With dessert consisting of Iced Plum, Cinnamon and Port Parfait with a Compote of Morello Cherries, you would have to be hungry indeed to do justice to the excellent cheeses and home-made biscuits that follow. If any particular courses do not appeal within the set menu, alternatives are available. Smoking is confined to the hotel's public rooms, with the exception of the restaurant. To complement menus the hotel carries a cellar book of nearly 300 wines starting in price from 'House', at around £10, to vintages of £20 or more.

In addition to Llangoed Hall's own all-weather tennis court and croquet lawn, there are opportunities for salmon and trout fishing on the Upper Wye and Irfon rivers. Shooting and riding are available locally, and for walkers and riders, the Brecon Beacons have plentiful possibilities. If less energetic pursuits are more to your liking, the hotel's chauffeur-driven car is available for private hire at all times.

As well as leisure pursuits, there are a considerable number of places of interest not far from the hotel. Hay-on-Wye, famous for its antiquarian bookshops, is nine miles away. Wordsworth's beloved Tintern Abbey, and Chepstow Castle lie to the southeast; while nearby Hereford – with its Cathedral and Mappa Mundi – or the fifteenth-century Raglan Castle are fascinating, if sometimes heavily tourist-frequented sites.

43

MAES-Y-NEUADD

Address Talsarnau, near Harlech, Gwynedd, North
Wales LL47 6YA
Tel: 0766 780200 Fax: 0766 780211

Nearest town Harlech
Directions Drive north from Harlech on the B4573.
The hotel is about three miles along this road,
between Harlech and the village of Talsarnau. A
large sign directs guests to a winding lane which
goes on for about half a mile.
Associate of the **Welsh Rarebits** group of
independent hotels of distinction, and **Pride of
Britain**
Awards AA *** graded; Egon Ronay and Michelin
recommended.
Open throughout the year, except between 9 and
19 December.
Special breaks Winter breaks from October until
April; discounts for half-board stays of two days or
more.
Price for dinner, with wine, bed and breakfast for
two – £100–£150

Credit cards Access and Visa.
The hotel is suitable for disabled visitors; children under seven are accepted only at the management's discretion; dogs are permitted.
Overall mark out of ten 7½

The rather isolated north Wales location of the Maes-y-Neuadd hotel is one of its more obvious attractions. Pronounced 'Mice-er-nayath', which means 'the hall in the field', the oldest part of the present building was completed around 1350. The first addition to the main structure was completed in 1550, and the final wing added in 1720, meaning that no part of the present hotel is less than two and a half centuries old. The main house and all the surrounding buildings, including the cottage and stable block, are built entirely from Welsh granite and slate.

For over 500 years the house belonged to the Nanney Wynn family, and a few surviving descendants still live nearby. Maes-y-Neuadd is reputed to have been used by Oliver Cromwell's forces during the English Civil War while he was laying siege to Harlech Castle. The house never featured prominently in Welsh history, although a number of the Wynn family rose to senior ranks in the army and government service and this is mentioned frequently in ancient poetry.

The family finally sold the house in 1953 and it was owned for a short spell by the Evans family. Margaret Evans has since written two books, one of which, *The Hall in the Field*, recounts her colourful life as a hotelier at Maes-y-Neuadd. Her second title, *The Wild Sky*, is a biographical novel featuring an interesting member of the Wynn family who flourished in the eighteenth century. The hotel today is owned and run by two families, June and Michael Slatter, and Olive and Malcolm Horsfall.

The main bar offers perhaps the best glimpse of what the inside of the house was really like a couple of centuries ago when it was one of the principal private homes in Gwynedd. Enormous dark oak beams have witnessed centuries of history and now provide a reassuring backdrop to the more traditional dark brown leather Chesterfields and roaring log fire on colder days throughout the autumn and winter. The other public room is a bright, informal lounge with sweeping views across the gardens and far beyond across Tremadoc Bay to the Lleyn Peninsula.

The hotel has sixteen bedrooms; thirteen doubles or twin rooms, one single and two suites. All the rooms have private bathroom facilities and each has a very individual style of decor. The hotel's colour brochure illustrates one of the premier rooms which is furnished with elegant Georgian-style windows and hanging dormer above twin beds. Recently, the coach house at Maes-y-Neuadd has been converted into luxurious accommodation, its two upstairs rooms incorporating beams within their high, sloping ceilings. As with the hotel itself, this accommodation is suitable for the disabled.

The focal point of the hotel is its restaurant, a gracious room with seating for up to forty guests at any one time. The style of cooking is modern British, although there are always a number of traditional Welsh dishes on the menu. Decor is Georgian, with a soft green and grey colour-scheme enhanced by light gold silk on the wall panels. This style is in keeping with the period in which this 'younger' part of the house was built.

Under Head Chef Andrew Taylor, the cuisine of Maes-y-Neuadd leans towards French in style. Starters include Trout, Mussel and Langoustine Terrine wrapped in Spinach with Orange and Champagne Jelly. Main-dish in-house specialities include Escallops of Salmon served with Smoked Scallops in a Caviar Sauce, and Roast Saddle of Venison Provençale with a Honey Sauce. All main courses are accompanied by a selection of fresh vegetables grown locally. A moderately priced wine list is available with a good range of mainly younger European wines to suit most palates.

Nearby attractions are plentiful and include a string of historic castles of which the best known is Harlech. The renowned Royal St David's golf course is just three miles away, and there are a number of gorgeous beaches and quaint little resorts all along the north-west Welsh coast.

44

PALÉ HALL

Address Llandderfel, Bala, Gwynedd, North Wales
LL23 7PS
Tel: 06783 285

Nearest town Bala.
Directions From north Wales, follow A5104 to
Corwen. At a large T-junction and traffic lights a
sign will indicate Llangollen A494 on your left. Turn
left here over the bridge and immediately turn
right signposted Llandrillo B4401. From here it is
eight and a half miles to Palé gates.
Awards AA *** RAC graded; Egon Ronay and
Michelin recommended.
Open throughout the year.
Price for dinner, with wine, bed and breakfast for
two – £150–£200
Credit cars Access, Visa, Amex and Diners.
*Children are allowed; dogs are only allowed at the
discretion of the management – but not in the bedrooms.*
Overall mark out of ten 8½

Almost everything about Palé Hall represents an elegant reminder of the late Victorian era when the house flourished as a private home. The house has only been a hotel for a few years, and resident proprietors Tim and Jain Ovens have worked hard to restore the old house to something approaching its former glory. They have managed to combine period luxury with discreet personal service making this, now, one of the most comfortable hotels in north Wales.

Palé Hall was built in 1870 by a Scottish gentleman, Henry Robertson, who rose to become one of Britain's principal railway engineers by the end of the last century, and who gave the architects unlimited resources for the construction of the house. He was responsible for laying the North Wales Mineral Railway and for the construction of a number of important bridges, including the iron Kingsland Toll Bridge near Shrewsbury in 1879. He twice served as the Liberal Member of Parliament for Shrewsbury, from 1860 to 1865 and again from 1874 (after the introduction of the secret ballot in British elections) until 1885. Once he'd firmly settled into Palé Hall, he served briefly as MP for Meirionyddshire after 1885, but left the Liberal Party in disgust after falling out with Gladstone over the old Prime Minister's controversial proposals for Irish Home Rule. He died suddenly in March 1888 after suffering a paralysing stroke at Palé Hall, and is buried at nearby Llandderfel.

Robertson's son Henry was knighted by Queen Victoria, and he invited her to Palé Hall as his guest in 1889. She stayed a few nights in a plush suite which is now open to residents, and both an identical half-tester bed, and the very bath which she used during her stay can be enjoyed by residents who have booked early enough to secure the Victoria Suite. Her Majesty, understandably, was said to have been 'enchanted' by Palé Hall and thoroughly enjoyed what was to be her only visit during her long reign. In the present century, the house served as a military hospital during both world wars.

The hotel's main public room, then as now, is a small, but truly magnificent, domed lounge with an intricate hand-painted ceiling, rich with gold leaf and ornate paintwork. With its comfortable blue velvet-covered suite and enormous bay windows offering wide views across the surrounding grounds, this room really is a delight. In order to preserve the delicate decor, there is a strict smoking ban as, indeed, there is in the main dining-room for the same reason. The other public room is the Corwen Bar, an interesting place to relax and enjoy an aperitif before dinner as the bar has been made from a number of old marble fireplaces. This isn't instantly obvious and tends to strike most guests as they sit back in their Roman-style bar chairs and study the room's decor in some detail.

The style of cooking at Palé Hall is traditional British Country House, and seldom more than 10 per cent of diners are non-residents. Italian carved dining chairs are upholstered in gold, and huge ornate mirrors adorn the walls all around. An impressive à la carte menu is available offering a strong range of fish and local poultry; an interesting starter is the Hot Prawn Soufflé with Mushroom Cream Sauce, garnished with Shrimp Tails. For most guests, though, the table d'hôte menu is more than adequate. One fish dish stands out: Trio of Fish, including salmon, trout and whiting, is served poached in Noilly Prat and coated with Shellfish Sauce. The wine list is reasonable but has no outstanding varieties. House wines are particularly palatable, at around £7 a bottle, but if you prefer something a little more adventurous then few of the vintages reach £20.

The hotel has seventeen bedrooms, all doubles except for one single, and all with private bathroom facilities. Little extras like a bowl of fruit, a jar of peppermints and a selection of drinks to greet you, are pleasing. One particular luxury double/suite – the Caernarfon Room – represents superb value at around £125 for two inclusive of bed and breakfast and a private jacuzzi in your room.

Leisure facilities at Palé Hall are excellent: there are two golf courses as well as a riding centre. Nearby, fishing can be arranged in the rivers Dee and Tryweryn as well as in Bala Lake; also clay pigeon and game shooting; and even rapid-riding and windsurfing for the young at heart. The hotel advises that both can be a little wet!

Nearby attractions, other than the impressive range of leisure facilities, include Harlech Castle and the surrounding beauty of Snowdonia, Shell Island (Mochras), a man-made island formed in 1819, and the seaside resort town of Barmouth.

RUTHIN CASTLE

Address Ruthin, Clwyd, Wales LL15 2NU
Tel: 08242 2664 Fax: 08242 5978

Nearest town Ruthin.
Directions From the town of Chester, Ruthin Castle
is located 22 miles south-west of Chester on the
A494 Ruthin to Corwen road, just off the
roundabout in the village of Ruthin.
A member of the **Best Western Hotels** consortium.
Awards AA *** RAC graded; British Tourist
Authority Services to Tourism Award 1979.
Open throughout the year.
Special breaks Getaway breaks for two days or
longer are available all year.
Price for dinner, with wine, bed and breakfast for
two – £100–£150.
Credit cards Access, Visa, Amex and Diners.
*The hotel is suitable for disabled visitors; children and
dogs are welcome.*
Overall mark out of ten 8

Situated twenty-two miles south-west of Chester, one of Norman England's marcher lordships, Ruthin Castle has probably the finest historical pedigree of any Welsh Country House Hotel. When Reginald de Grey had Ruthin Castle built in 1282 he created not only a magnificent new castle, but also the genesis of an entire community. Officials, retainers, craftsmen, domestic servants and a great many others were brought to Ruthin to maintain and build up de Grey's little empire. For their immediate security a wall was raised round what soon became a small town, and a huge stone gate was erected to make sure only those travellers friendly to the great lord entered the community.

Many features of the original thirteenth-century castle can be seen today: the early English-style west gate, with grooves for the portcullis; the postern gate with a spiral staircase contained within seven- to nine-foot-thick stone walls; and the slanted apertures in the battlements for the bowmen. Parts of the original castle form the shell of the modern-day hotel, but most of the original fortress, which was substantially bigger than the hotel, lies in rather poignant ruin around the main residential building.

The castle endured many attacks down the centuries, particularly during the Wars of the Roses, but the de Grey family remained in the castle until 1508. It passed briefly into the hands of Henry VIII's bastard son, Henry Fitzroy, but its darkest day came during the English Revolution when its Royalist inhabitants were routed and the castle dismantled. Ruthin remained a derelict ruin until the nineteenth century, when much of it was lovingly rebuilt, and a century later – in 1963 – it finally became a luxury Country House Hotel.

With such an outstanding history, guests at Ruthin are thankfully not allowed to forget the heritage which grew up within its four walls. A splendid medieval banquet evening is available, and this is a tremendously entertaining night out which you really shouldn't miss for one night of your stay here. Food is served on large wooden bowls and eaten with the fingers, and accompanied by generous gobletfuls of wine and local mead.

All the public rooms in Ruthin Castle are furnished on a grand scale, and the main reception area is decorated in a traditional style with deer antlers and ancient firearms adorning the walls. Virtually all public rooms have an ornate criss-cross ceiling pattern – a nightmare to decorate but magnificent to admire as you relax in comfortable chairs with an after-dinner liqueur or coffee.

The hotel is one of the largest featured in this book, with fifty-eight spacious and sound-proofed bedrooms, all with private bathroom facilities, colour television and direct-dial telephone. Recently, thirty-two of the bedrooms have been refurnished to a high standard. Ruthin Castle is a particularly popular venue for both 'society' weddings and business conferences and seminars. The huge Peacock Room is glass-walled on three sides and allows a terrific amount of natural light to flood in.

The restaurant is an attractive, long dining room decorated in greens and browns with grand arrays of dried flowers in opposite corners. When full, it can seat up to a hundred people and the ratio of residents to non-residents varies enormously throughout the year. That said, it is seldom necessary to book more than a day or so in advance if you wish to dine as a non-resident. The menu concentrates on British Country House specialities, but there is a strong continental influence in the à la carte menu which represents excellent value at under £20 per person, including a selection from the modest wine list.

A strong range of starters includes a delicious Marinated Frogs' Legs speciality, cooked with different sorts of Mushrooms and served in a Garlic and Oregano Butter. For a more unusual soup, Ruthin offers an impressive Turtle variety topped with a Curry Flavoured Cream. Main course options are equally strong on both poultry and red meat dishes. An outstanding speciality, cooked in front of you, is Steak Diane: this huge, flattened entrecôte steak is sautéed in Butter, Mushrooms and Red Wine and served Brandy-flamed. The sauce is exquisite. For a special luxury dish, few will need to look further than the chef's Futtora Piccata: thin slices of fillet beef, sautéed in butter and served with Mushrooms, Onions and Potatoes.

Nearby attractions include Caernarfon Castle, Conwy Castle, the city of Chester, Bodnant Gardens and the splendid National Trust properties of Erddig Hall and Chirk Castle.

Central England

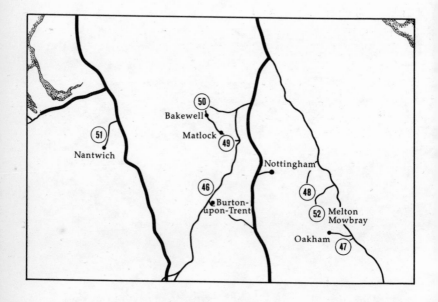

Central England

46

BROOKHOUSE INN

Address Brookside, Rolleston-on-Dove, near
Burton-on-Trent, Staffordshire DE13 9AA
Tel: 0283 814188

Nearest town Burton-on-Trent.
Directions From the north, travel via the A38 from
Derby towards Rolleston; from the south, head out
of Birmingham, on the same road. The turn-off for
the village of Rolleston is clearly signposted and
the hotel is located in the village.
Awards British Tourist Authority commended;
Ashley Courtenay recommended.
Open from mid-January until Christmas Eve.
Special **weekend breaks** are available throughout
the year from dinner Friday until breakfast Sunday.
Price for dinner, with wine, bed and breakfast for
two – under £100.
Credit cards Access, Visa, Amex and Diners.

Children under the age of ten are not catered for; dogs are allowed.
Overall mark out of ten 7

The Brookhouse Inn is hidden in the quiet Staffordshire village of Rolleston-on-Dove, and offers the luxurious tranquillity you would expect of a Country House Hotel with the added charm of a typical rural English village. Originally a farmhouse, the hotel was built during the brief joint reign of William and Mary at the end of the seventeenth century. It had an undistinguished history until recently.

A programme of renovation and decoration has resulted in a relaxed and informal little hotel, not a Country House in the strictest sense because of its village location, but more than fitting the comfort standards associated with Country House Hotels. From the moment you approach the hotel you will be struck by its solid exterior. It was built in the generation which immediately preceded the elaborate Georgian era of English architecture and its symmetrical window pattern, with small frames and brilliant white paintwork, contrasts starkly with the red brickwork.

The hotel's main public room is a large reception lounge, its red and black carpet enhancing the bare brickwork of a couple of the walls. Blue and white china candelabras are crafted in a design similar to old brass lanterns, and give a glimpse of what life might have been like at the Brookhouse Inn in former years. Perhaps the proprietors have tried a little too hard to recreate the period feel in this room as the imposing old fireplace is almost groaning with china plates and antique trinkets.

The bedrooms at Brookhouse are a delight. Each one is individually furnished in a period with huge overhead wooden beams, swirling curtains and matching counterpanes. Most of the double bedrooms have huge four-poster beds and are furnished with authentic chairs and dressing tables. The gentle aroma of Victorian-style pot pourri is a pleasing touch.

There are nineteen bedrooms in all, plus one suite, and eight of the rooms are in the main farmhouse building. The remainder are in the carefully renovated old barn. All bedrooms have private bathroom facilities, with a number of little extras like exclusive soaps, talcum, shampoo, foam bath, crystals and even a thoughtful glass of detergents for emergency washing. As an added concession to modern comfort, colour television and telephones are included in all bedrooms.

One of the principal attractions of the Brookhouse Inn is its high standard of cooking. The dining room promises an atmosphere of homely elegance and evening meals are served on the finest Staffordshire bone china. The room feels rather small, but this lends a sense of intimacy rather than crampedness. You sit at antique tables laid with heavy silver plate and cut crystal while Head Chef David Bould takes charge of the cooking. Twice weekly trips to Birmingham ensure that all produce for the Brookhouse table is fresh and of the highest quality. The menu has few surprises at first glance, but you will quickly discover that virtually all main dish choices are enhanced by unique speciality sauces from the Brookhouse kitchen. A few interesting French dishes pop up amid the more standard English Country House-style menu, including Snails on the range of starters and Breasts of French Duck stuffed with Chicken Mousse on the list of main dishes.

Lobster is generally available, prepared in a Cream, Wine and Mustard Sauce, glazed in its shell with cheese, and a good buy at around £15 per head. All main course dishes include vegetables, a sensible addition which, more often than not, comes as an extra few pounds on your bill. Brookhouse boasts a comprehensive wine cellar which includes a number of more unusual foreign vintages.

Nearby attractions include the towns of Burton-on-Trent, Stafford, Derby and Stoke-on-Trent together with the city of Birmingham. Golf and fishing can be arranged nearby, and for a relaxing walk you won't need to look further than the Brookhouse's country garden – complete with English brook flowing through.

47

HAMBLETON HALL

Address Hambleton, Oakham, Rutland LE15 8TH
Tel: 0572 756991

Nearest town Oakham.
Directions From the south, take the A606 towards
Oakham. Approximately one mile before Oakham
look for the (signposted) left turn to Hambleton
village only. About 2.5 miles down this road is the
village itself and the hotel is on the right at the end
of the village.
A member of the **Relais et Châteaux** consortium.
Awards AA *** (red) graded and rosette for food;
AA award for Best Welcome 1985; Michelin three
(red) Turrets and rosette for food; Egon Ronay 82%
and award Hotel of the Year 1985; Egon Ronay
Cellar of the Year 1986; *Good Hotel Guide* César
Award for comprehensive excellence in the Luxury
class 1985; Badoit and *Decanter* magazine Restaurant
of the Year 1987.
Open throughout the year.
Special breaks Winter breaks available November
until April.

Price for dinner, with wine, bed and breakfast, for two – over £150.
Credit cards Access and Visa.
The hotel is suitable for disabled guests; children and dogs accepted by prior arrangement.
Overall mark out of ten 9

Tim and Stefa Hart opened Hambleton Hall as a hotel in 1980. When they did so, they had a keen desire to retain the Hambleton style of English country living which had distinguished it in the century or so before, when it was a private residence. The house was built in 1881 by Walter Marshall as a base for his hunting activities with a number of local fox hunts. Marshall never married, is remembered for the excellence of his dinner table and cellar, and the somewhat generous level of female company he kept at Hambleton.

His younger sister, Mrs Eva Astley Paston Cooper, inherited the house after his death and became quite a socialite in her day. Well-known figures such as Noël Coward, Charles Scott-Moncrieff and Sir Malcolm Sargent are all known to have visited Hambleton Hall at least once. The house had various owners prior to 1980, and although the interior had undergone few fundamental changes since the last century, the whole country-side around Hambleton Hall changed markedly in 1976 with the creation of Rutland Water. Acres of land were deliberately flooded, creating what is now a rather picturesque man-made reservoir and lake.

One of Hambleton Hall's most attractive rooms is the main dining room, a bright restaurant decorated by internationally known interior designer Nina Campbell and with a seating capacity for up to fifty people. The views far across Rutland Water are wonderful and would almost convince you that the great lake has always been a natural feature of the land. The cuisine at Hambleton is extremely popular with residents and non-residents alike, and the proprietors advise that up to a month's notice is generally required for non-residents wishing to dine here on a Saturday evening. For other nights, try to allow at least a week's warning.

Chef Brian Baker's style of cooking has been highlighted by an impressive number of guide books. Clear and exciting flavours are the hallmark of a number of dishes and presentation is always appealing without being overfussy. The daily-changed menu is impressive: an ornate rectangular card, designed by artist Hugh Robson, it looks more like a family tree plan at first glance than a menu. And, as in the best family trees, you can be assured of a few interesting surprises as you read through it.

A set table d'hôte menu is available each evening, but to appreciate the luxury cuisine offered by Hambleton Hall you would be well advised to glance through the à la carte dishes before making up your mind. Favourite starters include a Vinaigrette of Baby Vegetables with a Mousse of Pea and Mint which in winter becomes a Root Artichoke Mousse with Baby Onions and Raisins. Sea Bass is cooked with an Aubergine Terrine and slightly garlicky Provençal vegetables and main courses feature game in winter and, year round, a delicious Pavé Steak served with crisply fried Shredded Leeks, Carrots and Courgettes. Whatever your choice, there is an extensive wine list which is pretty well guaranteed to include your favourite bottle. As the proprietors themselves admit, the wine list concentrates on bottles which are excellent to drink rather than a worthy accumulation of fashionable labels with indifferent contents.

The hotel has fifteen bedrooms, all with private facilities, colour television and telephone, and most with great views across Rutland Water and beyond. There is also a lift to all floors.

A helpful booklet, updated annually, is given to all guests and outlines a host of things to do around Hambleton Hall. A number of recreation facilities are available at the hotel, including trout fishing, sailing, riding, tennis, golf and shooting. A rather unusual recreation, fox hunting, is unlikely to be to everyone's taste, but can be arranged for guests keen to try this sport of the English upper classes.

Nearby attractions include Belvoir (pronounced 'beaver')

Castle, Althorp (home of the Earl and Countess Spencer, father and stepmother of the Princess of Wales), Lincoln, Stamford, Boughton, Burghley and Belton.

48

LANGAR HALL

Address Langar, Nottinghamshire NG13 9HG
Tel: 0949 60559

Nearest town Nottingham.
Directions Langar Hall is located twenty miles
south of Leicester, and is signposted off the main
A46 Leicester to Newark road via Cropwell Bishop,
or else off the A52 Grantham to Nottingham road.
A member of the **Wolsey Lodges and Country
Homes** group.
Open throughout the year, except weekends in
January and February when the hotel is open by
arrangement only to groups of four or more.
No **special breaks** available, although private
parties can be accommodated.
Price for dinner, with wine, bed and breakfast for
two – £100–£150.
Credit cards Access, Visa and Diners.

The hotel is not suitable for the disabled; children are
allowed but dogs are permitted only by prior arrangement,
unless their owner is staying in the Parachute Suite.
Overall mark out of ten 7

Langar Hall is one of those places which seem to have been forgotten by the outside world. Apart from *Johansen's* and *Hotel Directory*, few other guides, even the normally thorough AA, acknowledge the existence of this little hotel, and for guests who are attracted by a secluded atmosphere this is one of the most positive features of Langar Hall. The hotel is the ideal base for exploring most of the southern English shires, and a comfortable stop for travellers heading from north to south, or vice versa.

The house is unobtrusive, with the emphasis on comfort and privacy rather than pampered luxury, and even the history of the present late Georgian house is rather undistinguished. Yet there is something about Langar Hall which, for many, makes it simply irresistible. It was built in 1830 on the site of a great house, and was for a while home to Admiral Lord Howe who was the hero of the 'Glorious 1st of June' English naval victory in 1794.

All of the public rooms and bedrooms enjoy fine views across ancient parkland and a veritable maze of medieval fish ponds. Surrounding Langar Hall, the gardens provide the basis for a number of entertaining short walks of varying length, depending on how much energy you have to spare.

This hotel is different in so many ways that it is rather difficult to use the same objective criteria by which virtually every other hotel in this guide has been described. Suffice it to say that it offers rather more than an informal welcome: guests are all treated like personal friends of the resident owner Imogen Skirving. Throughout your stay at Langar Hall you will be able to appreciate her unique combination of the standards of a good hotel with the hospitality of Country House living. As she herself is proud to admit, this enjoyable experience is 'delightfully different'.

In summer, guests use the White Drawing Room, a marvellous old Adam-style parlour with comfortable armchairs and a wide collection of local guide books and magazines for guests to browse through or ignore just as they could in their own homes. In winter, the main public room is the library with its welcoming log fire.

The walls offer a veritable art gallery of nineteenth-century to modern paintings, and if one happens to take your fancy then you can even take it home as they are exhibited for sale.

There is a choice of around six starter dishes and a similar number of main-course meals. At £20, this certainly represents good value for money. On a number of occasions, Theme Theatre Dinners are available, where short plays are performed after dinner: an excellent way to round off Marinated Wild Boar in Red Wine and Juniper Berries, or Medallion of Monkfish with fresh Chive Butter. Menus are flexible to suit guests, and all fall into the category of 'imaginative' British Country House style.

Langar Hall has ten bedrooms, three of which are double: the Brownlow, with its old four-poster, overlooks the park; the Edwards is a larger double with a solid half-tester-style bed and views across the park and moats; and the Charlotte is a twin-bedded room overlooking the garden. All three have private bathroom facilities, colour television and tea- and coffee-making facilities. In the adjoining Coach House, the Parachute Suite has a double-bedded room with adjoining twin-bed sitting room and kitchenette, making it ideal for families with children.

Nearby attractions include Belvoir Castle, Belton House, Doddington Hall, Southwell Minster, Newstead Abbey, Sherwood Forest (where Robin Hood once roamed) and the beautiful city of Nottingham. The stately home of the dukes of Devonshire, Chatsworth, is less than an hour's drive away.

49

RIBER HALL

Address Matlock, Derbyshire DE4 5JU
Tel: 0629 582795 Fax: 0629 580475

Nearest town Matlock.
Directions Leave the M1 at junction 28 and follow
the A38/A615 signposted for Matlock. The hotel is
about a mile south-east of the town, just off the
main road at Tansley.
A member of the **Pride of Britain** consortium.
Awards AA *** graded; British Tourist Authority
commended.
Open all year.
Winter breaks are available from mid-October until
April.
Price for dinner, with wine, bed and breakfast for
two – £100–£150.
Credit cards All major cards accepted.
*The hotel is unsuitable for the disabled; children under
ten and dogs are not allowed.*
Overall mark out of ten 9

Few other British Country House Hotels can offer a more tranquil setting than the edge of the Peak District National Park – and at the same time offer the accessibility of the M1 just twenty minutes away, as well as a number of large towns within half an hour's drive.

Riber Hall hotel was effectively rescued from a derelict shell in 1970, but its origins lie far back in the fifteenth century when it was built by the Riberghs of Riber. By marriage, the house passed through a couple of generations of Robothams, and then the Wolley family, who lived here for a further seven generations until 1668. The most recent structural addition to the house was undertaken by the last of the Wolleys, in 1661, seven years before Riber Hall passed out of the family's hands for good.

Three centuries followed, and gradually the old house fell into a state of disuse which progressed to near dereliction. Only the huge commitment of current owners Alex and Gill Biggin when they bought the house nearly twenty years ago saved Riber Hall, and the magnificent results of their devotion to the huge task of restoring and refurbishing can be seen today.

Beamed ceilings dominate virtually all rooms inside Riber Hall. The main public room, apart from the dining room, is a long lounge which has the hotel's most striking ceiling. Deep brushed velvet armchairs complement a number of upright antique chairs placed around the enormous carved fireplace, and the little touches like the grandfather clock in one corner, and the old post horn above the main doorway, make it a place of immense character.

The dining room is a striking early Georgian-style room, with two huge white cross-beams dominating the ceiling and authentic Jacobean and Adam fireplaces. The decor reflects a different period in the history of Riber Hall, making a rather unusual combination of furnishings, but, nevertheless, creating a very unique and pleasing effect. Dark wood period furniture contrasts well with the light wall decor, and the heavy crystal glass, silver cutlery and fan-folded linen napkins complete the intimate period feel.

The style of cuisine is a combination of French *nouvelle* and classical, and Riber Hall has long been acknowledged as an outstanding restaurant in this part of England. Up to fifty can be seated at once, but advance booking is essential for non-residents. There is a fine à la carte menu working out at around £25 per person, inclusive of service and VAT, and there is a strong emphasis on the best local produce, particularly game. The wine list is outstandingly compiled and comprehensive, with some keenly priced younger European vintages available, as well as a good selection of exclusive wines.

Riber Hall has eleven bedrooms, all of which offer exceptionally high standards of comfort. All the rooms have a very individual decor: it could be Tudor red, or a gentle blend of pastel shades, but you are unlikely to be disappointed by the clever interior design displayed throughout the hotel. Most rooms still have a number of old support beams blended into the decor of the room, and one or two have the added period touch of authentic stonework on at least one of the walls. In addition to very smart private bathroom facilities, nine rooms have antique four-poster beds and five have that most favoured luxury, a private jacuzzi. All the rooms are large, airy and extremely comfortable. Probably the highest compliment that can be paid to any Country House Hotel is that it doesn't 'feel' like a hotel. Riber Hall definitely falls into that category, as you will doubtless discover as soon as you enter one of the bedrooms.

Nearby attractions include a number of outstanding stately homes and castles within half an hour's drive. The best of these is Chatsworth House, family home of the Duke and Duchess of Devonshire, but others include Sudbury Hall, Haddon Hall and Hardwick Hall. The Peak National Park is about fifteen minutes away, and of the surrounding towns and villages the most obvious targets for visitors to the area are Derby and Nottingham.

50

RIVERSIDE

Address Fennel Street, Ashford-in-the-Water,
Bakewell, Derbyshire DE4 1QF
Tel: 062981 4275

Nearest town Bakewell.
Directions From Bakewell, follow the A6 for about
two miles to the village of Ashford-in-the-Water. The
hotel is at the top of the main street.
Awards British Tourist Authority commended;
English Tourist Board four Crowns; recommended in
Egon Ronay and Michelin guides.
Open throughout the year.
Bargain breaks for two nights or longer; half-board
is available all year.
Price for dinner, with wine, bed and breakfast for
two – £100–£150.
Credit cards Access, Visa and Amex.
*The hotel is not suitable for the disabled; children are
welcome, by arrangement; only small dogs allowed, and
then by prior arrangement at the proprietors' discretion.*
Overall mark out of ten 7½

Situated in the middle of the Peak District National Park, the Riverside Country House lies amid an array of quaint cottages in the attractive little Derbyshire hamlet of Ashford-in-the-Water. The hotel has an ageless feeling about it, and is set in an acre of mature garden with much of its exterior covered by dense green ivy. The gardens lead down to the River Wye, and there can be few more peaceful pre-dinner strolls in this part of northern England than the short walk from the rear of the hotel down to the water's edge.

Parts of the main building date back to the mid-seventeenth century, but it is essentially a typical Georgian-style Country House. Resident proprietors Roger and Sue Taylor take pride in the attentive personal service on offer at the Riverside. Both dining rooms, the sitting room and the cocktail bar are tastefully furnished in a traditional modern decor which, refreshingly, has not tried to emulate any given period style, with the result that guests can sit back and relax in timeless comfort. The main sitting room has long windows and, with a view that stretches down to the river, overlooks the garden.

Great care has been taken, however, to ensure that all the hotel's original beams, together with the polished oak panelling which adorns most of the public area, have been carefully preserved and looked after. Roger Taylor himself has taken charge of all the recent renovation work to ensure that the comfortable and elegant interior which distinguished the house when it was a private residence is altered as little as possible.

There are two dining rooms, both furnished with polished antique tables, and the main restaurant can seat up to forty, of which a maximum of fourteen are residents at any one time. A Regency-style crystal chandelier dominates the room, and the use of silver cutlery and quality chinaware enhances the exceptionally high standard of cuisine at the Riverside. This is one of the most popular places to eat out in northern England, so advance booking by at least a week or two really is essential.

The ever-changing menu is very imaginatively presented, and the style, though distinctly *nouvelle cuisine*, has refreshingly British-sized portions. Two favourite starters are Fresh Mushrooms Stuffed with home-made Duck Liver Pâté, deep fried in batter; and fresh Chilled Watermelon dusted with Ground Black Pepper served with Quenelles of home-made Smoked Salmon Sorbet and garnished with Lemon and Cucumber.

Main dishes are no less imaginative and include Carved Roast Breast of Goose, stretched out on a bed of Crispy Stuffing made from Apples, Sultanas, Bacon and Thyme, all complemented by a tangy Juniper Berry Sauce garnished with Segments of Citrus Fruits. If local game is a dish you enjoy, then one of chef Jeremy Buckingham's favourite dishes is a delicious combination of rabbit, hare, pheasant, steak and kidney all cooked in Guinness and topped in pastry before being served with a rich gravy.

At present the hotel has fifteen bedrooms, eleven individually styled doubles, two twins and two singles. The bedrooms really are a delight, each one with its own antique bed, and a number have either four-posters or half-testers which are draped in fine Nottingham lace. All have private bathroom facilities, complete with antique brass and gold fittings, together with the more modern conveniences of colour television, direct-dial telephones and high-quality furnishings.

The Riverside really is an ideal place to escape to for that special break. The hotel doesn't go overboard with special sporting facilities, but if you are keen to indulge in some gentle exercise then golf, fishing, shooting and guided walks can be arranged quite easily. For nature lovers the Peak District National Park is all around, but other nearby attractions include Chatsworth, the stately home of the Duke and Duchess of Devonshire, Haddon Hall, Hardwick Hall and the historic city of Derby forty miles away.

51

ROOKERY HALL

Address Worleston, near Nantwich, Cheshire CW5
6DQ
Tel: 0270 626866

Nearest town Nantwich.
Directions Approaching from the south, on the M6,
exit at junction 16 and turn left to follow the A500
Nantwich road. Go over the level crossing and turn
right at the roundabout taking the A51 past two
sets of traffic lights. Take the next right turn on the
B5074 to Worleston and this will take you to
Rookery Hall after one and a half miles.
A member of **Select Country Hotels Ltd**.
Awards AA *** (red) graded and rosette for food;
RAC *** graded and Blue Ribbon; Egon Ronay and
Michelin recommended; 1986 *Sunday Times* Sunday
Lunch Restaurant of the Year.
Open throughout the year.
Special **winter breaks** are available from 1 October
until 31 March.

Price for dinner, with wine, bed and breakfast for two – over £200.
Credit cards All major cards accepted.
The hotel is suitable for disabled guests; children under ten and dogs are not allowed.
Overall mark out of ten 9½

If the generous praise heaped on to Rookery Hall by assorted hotel and catering organizations and other independent guide books is anything to go by, this particular hotel has managed to attain one of the best reputations of any Country House Hotel in central England. The hotel is set amid 200 acres of exquisite gardens and wooded parkland, and the care and attention which has so obviously been lavished on these is typical of the high standards you can expect inside the hotel as well. All praise *is* deserved and this is, undoubtedly, one of England's finest Country House Hotels.

Rookery Hall was built by William Hilton Cooke at the end of the eighteenth century. It changed hands in 1867 when Baron Von Schroder, a wealthy banker, bought it, and from then until his death shortly before the outbreak of the First World War he gradually changed the traditional Georgian mansion into the small château which you can see today. The external walls are of fine mellowed sandstone, although little remains of the original building, other than some fine plasterwork inside and the attractive marble chimneypiece which dominates the elegant salon lounge.

Wherever you go inside the hotel, there is a feeling of spaciousness. The main staircase is crafted from the finest English oak and gives a reassuring sense of grandeur as you sweep down to dinner dressed in your finery. The sitting room is the epitome of elegance and, on a breezy Sunday morning, there can be few more welcoming places to enjoy your morning coffee and a leisurely leaf through the Sunday papers.

But it is the restaurant which really stands out as a public room of great class, and it is one of the finest Victorian dining rooms in England. The walls are lined with highly polished mahogany and walnut panelling, and this is more than comp-